SUMAC

Anas Atassi

SUMAC
Recipes and Stories from Syria

Interlink Books

Table of Contents
—

(009)   Introduction
(013)   Welcome to my kitchen
(026)   Recipes

Breakfast

(025)   WEEKEND BREAKFAST IN MY GRANDMOTHER'S GARDEN

(026)   Musabaha—Chickpeas in Yogurt–Tahini Sauce
(029)   Jazmaz—Eggs in Tomato Sauce with Chilies
(030)   Man'oushe za'atar—Za'atar Flatbread
(033)   Foul mudammas—Fava Beans in Olive Oil
(034)   Murabba el-batinjan—Eggplant Jam
(037)   Ejjeh—Egg Pancakes with Parsley
(038)   Khebzeh harra—Flatbread with Spicy Tomato Sauce
(041)   Labneh—Yogurt Cheese
(042)   Labneh Balls

Mezze for Sharing and Spreading

(047)   MY MOTHER'S ANNUAL SOIRÉES

(048)   Moutabal—Roasted Eggplant, Yogurt, and Tahini Dip
(051)   Batersh—Roasted Eggplant Dip with Tomato–Meat Sauce
(052)   Mufarakeh—Eggs with Beef and Zucchini
(055)   Eggplant and Red Pepper Dip
(056)   Batata harra—Spicy Potatoes with Garlic and Cilantro
(060)   Hummus bi tahini—Hummus with Tahini
(061)   Hummus bi zeit—Hummus with Olive Oil
(064)   Foul ma'ala—Fresh Fava Beans with Cilantro and Garlic
(067)   Moutabal shawandar—Beet and Tahini Dip
(068)   Fatayer bi sabankh—Spinach Pies
(071)   Sambusak—Filo Rolls with Cheese Filling
(074)   Sambusak—Filo Rolls with Meat Filling
(075)   Sfeeha—Mini-Flatbreads with Ground Beef
(079)   Mortadella from Aleppo—Beef Sausage with Garlic and Pistachios
(080)   Laban bi khyar—Yogurt with Cucumber and Garlic
(083)   Muhammara—Spicy Red Pepper–Walnut Dip

Street Food

(087)   BOYS' NIGHT OUT

(088)   Batinjan bi hamud—Sour Roasted Eggplant

(092)   Falafel

(093)   Beef shawarma

(098)   Zahra—Spicy Roasted Cauliflower

(103)   Toshka—Toasted Sandwiches with Spicy Meat and Cheese

(104)   Lob el kossa—Pan-Fried Zucchini with Garlic and Mint

Grains, Vegetables, and More

(109)   WARM DISHES FOR A WINTER SPREAD

(112)   Fattoush—Famous Toasted Bread Salad

(115)   Fasolia bi zeit—Green Beans in Tomato and Olive Oil Sauce

(116)   Shorbat adas—Traditional Red Lentil Soup

(119)   Itsch salad—Aunt Jinan's Bulgur Salad

(120)   Mkhallal—Spicy Pickles

(123)   Sheikh mushatah—Grilled Eggplants with Yogurt Sauce

(124)   Horak osbao—Lentil and Pasta Stew with Tamarind and Pomegranate

(127)   Mom's Famous Beet Salad

(128)   Mujaddara—Lentil Pilaf with Caramelized Onions

(134)   Yalanji—Swiss Chard Rolls with Rice Filling

(135)   Biwaz—Simple Onion and Parsley Salad

Meat Dishes

(139)   MIDSUMMER BARBECUES

(142)   Sabankh bil roz—Stew of Spinach and Ground Beef

(145)   Bazela bil roz—Beef Stew with Green Peas

(146)   Mnazaleh batinjan—Baked Eggplants and Ground Beef in Tomato Sauce

(151)   Makloube—Eggplant and Beef Pilaf

(152)   Lahme bi sayniyi—Lamb Koftas in Tahini Sauce

(156)   Kibbeh—Bulgur and Meat Croquettes

(159)   Kibbeh hamoud—Kibbeh in Sour Tomato-Pomegranate Sauce

(160)   Kibbeh laban—Kibbeh in Mint-Yogurt Sauce

(163)   Kibbeh sayniyi—Kibbeh Tart

(166)   Mahshi el jazar—Stuffed Parsnips in Tomato Sauce

(169)   Shorbat ameh—Tomato Soup with Barley and Lamb Shanks

(170)   Ouzi—Filo Pastries with Meat and Rice Filling

(173)   Kebab karaz—Lamb Kebabs with Cherries

(174)   Lamb and Vegetable Kebabs with Khebzeh Hamra

Chicken and Fish Dishes

(179)   THE TABLE OVERLOOKING THE SEA

(181)   Jambari ma'ala—Shrimp with Garlic, Cilantro, and Cayenne Pepper

(182)   Tajen samak—Fish with Sumac-Tahini Sauce

(187)   AGHABANI TABLECLOTHS

(188)   Sayadiyah—Spiced Fish Pilaf with Caramelized Onions

(191)   Chicken Kofta Kebabs

(194)   Shish tawook—Chicken Shish Kebabs

(197)   Red bulgur bi jara—"Dirty" Bulgur with Roast Chicken

(198)   Summer salad—Watermelon, Halloumi, and Mint Salad

(201)   Samke harra—Fish in Spicy Nut Sauce

(202)   Musakhan wraps—Flatbread with Chicken, Onions, and Sumac

Desserts and Beverages

(207)   THE RAMADAN TABLE

(210)   Qamar al-Deen—Apricot and Orange Blossom Juice with Pine Nuts

(213)   Mbatan—Rice Pudding with Apricot Syrup

(214)   Ashta—Syrian-Style Ricotta Cheese

(217)   Spiral shabiyat—Filo Spiral with Ashta and Raspberry Filling

(222)   Walnut baklava

(225)   Asafiri—Pancakes with Ashta and Pistachio Filling

(226)   Soos—Sweet-and-Sour Licorice Beverage

(229)   Jallab—Beverage with Molasses, Nuts, and Raisins

(230)   Karkadi—Sparkling Hibiscus Tea with Lemon Slices

(233)   Aish el saraya—Ashta and Caramel Bread "Cheesecake"

(234)   Karawiyah—Caraway Pudding with Nuts and Grated Coconut

(237)   Kaak—Cookies with a Sesame–Anise Glaze

(238)   Forgotten Date Cake

(241)   Qatayef—Mini-Pancakes with Ashta and Walnut Filling

(243)   Index
(247)   Acknowledgments

Introduction
—

As a child I was fascinated by television cooking shows and would spend hours watching them with my sister. It didn't matter if the chef was Italian, Asian, or Middle Eastern—there we were, glued to the TV. We would stage re-enactments of the shows (kitchen cabinets open for the full-size "television camera") and we were presenters of our very own cooking show, even if just momentarily. And, whenever I got the chance, I would sit in the kitchen to watch my mother cook, regaling her with my made-up stories in the hopes of being allowed to stay there just a little bit longer.

But it wasn't until I left home for my university studies that my love for cooking turned to Syrian cuisine. I missed those flavors; I missed the hospitality of my parents' home. So, in my attempts to stay connected to my home, my parents, and my homeland, I started to prepare my favorite foods.

It turned out that my culinary daydreaming, helped along with my mother's recipes, resulted in a tangible, edible way of reminiscing. I would send my mother pictures and she would return them with comments. That is how I learned, slowly but surely, how to make Syrian dishes myself. It was the physical distance that sparked my desire to understand the foundations of the traditional food of Syria, a desire that only grew greater; I even started to find charm in the boring old tablecloths (see page 187) that I had grown up with!

Even so, I'm not a chef. The recipes I make are my mother's recipes. And her recipes are, in large part, inherited from her mother. They've been passed down through time; they've been changed according to which ingredients were available in various countries and modified to fit the tastes of family and friends. They retain the heart of our family life in Syria—a family life shared by the majority of Syrians before the war cast us out and over the whole world.

This is why I share the stories of my family in this cookbook. They are not only my stories. They are the stories of an entire people—stories that are tied to our collective hearts, and have become all the more important because of the recent turmoil.

I was born in Homs, Syria, a city located between the country's two largest cities of Damascus and Aleppo. My parents moved to Saudi Arabia for work and so my sisters and I grew up outside Syria for most of our lives.

But, come summer, every year, we would travel back to Homs and celebrate. I say "celebrate" because that is how I continue to see Syria: as a place where life is to be cherished and enjoyed.

Our summers in Syria were marked by strings of parties—weddings, graduations, birthdays—each one with a table laden with all sorts of delicious treats. Even our normal, everyday meals tended to include a hint of the festive. Whether it was a weekend breakfast with our grandmother, a garden barbecue, or a late evening meal during Ramadan, eating well was what we shared. It is what bonded us together. With every passing summer those bonds grew tighter, and are preserved to this day, even though we live farther and farther apart from each other.

I prepare something Syrian at least once a day, even if it is as simple as a cookie with a cup of tea. And sometimes I eat Syrian food all day—for breakfast, lunch, and dinner. My friends don't find this hard to believe at all.

Syrian recipes, as shared throughout the world, are constantly adapting to the influences of other regions, so the recipes in this book cannot be thought of as pure and authentic. Time puts its stamp on a cuisine, and individual tastes and preferences also exert their influence. Even the most famous of dishes are subject to particular preparations in particular families. Take kibbeh hamoud (see page 159), for example. My mother's version is just a touch different from the kibbeh hamoud found in Aleppo, the region where it originated. She would, however, insist that we bring back as many packages and jars of ingredients as we could when we visited Syria, stuffing them between the clothes in our suitcases. That was how she would fill our pantry at the house in Saudi Arabia with authentic Syrian ingredients.

I've written my own personal preferences into some of this book's recipes. In some cases I will have eaten something on my travels that then combines nicely with a certain dish or that could be worked into a recipe. My red bulgur bi jara (see page 197) is a good example. It is originally Syrian, but with extra spices and peas added to it, inspired by way of a friend's "dirty rice" recipe. I haven't always been thanked for these twists on the traditional, but in the case of the bulgur, my mother did admit that she was impressed with the result.

Each of the recipes that follow remind me of the flavors, smells, and textures of Syrian cooking, no matter whether they are authentic throughout all of Syria or whether they are particular to a single region, village, or family. All of them deserve a place in this book.

There are, in my opinion, two indispensable ingredients in Syrian cooking. The first is one you cannot see or touch, though you can certainly taste it. It is called "nafas." Nafas literally means "breath," but in the context of cooking it means "the art of cooking where ingredients combine harmoniously." Nafas is the secret behind a good kaak (see page 237), an otherwise simple cookie with a likewise simple list of ingredients. Nafas is knowing how to get the best out of the season's harvest or how to use a perfectly ripe tomato. Nafas is the highest compliment you could possibly give to a Syrian cook. Nafas is found in the heart of the person at the stove and in the essence of a well-prepared dish. My grandmother has nafas. My mother has nafas. I hope that you, too, can find your nafas with the help of the recipes and stories contained in this book.

The second essential, and unmistakable, ingredient in Syrian cooking is sumac. Countless influences throughout the centuries have left their mark on Syrian cuisine, including the Ottoman Empire, the Persians, and the French. The Silk Road brought spices to Aleppo. Modern-day Syria borders six other countries, resulting in dishes that seem Mediterranean (in Tartus), that have Turkish or Armenian flavors (in Aleppo), or that are kept simple and subtle (in Damascus). But sumac. . . Sumac is used everywhere. This deep-red spice is, as they say in the Netherlands, the "red thread" that connects every dish. It is the red thread that will guide you through this book.

A lot has been done for us Syrians in recent years: from large projects carried out by humanitarian organizations to the housing of refugees throughout the world. The time has come for me, as a Syrian, to give something back. In December 2019, my Dutch publishing team and I hosted a charity dinner at Droog Gallery in Amsterdam. All the proceeds went to a Dutch-based NGO that strives to achieve a stable and loving environment for children who come from troubled families. As we launch this book in more and more countries, I would love to host similar charity dinners in your country to support local children's NGOs and cook delicious Syrian dishes. I don't have all the details worked out as yet for the next events and projects; follow me on Instagram @anasatassi for the latest as they take shape. Eat well and enjoy, from my table to yours!

Anas

WELCOME TO
MY KITCHEN

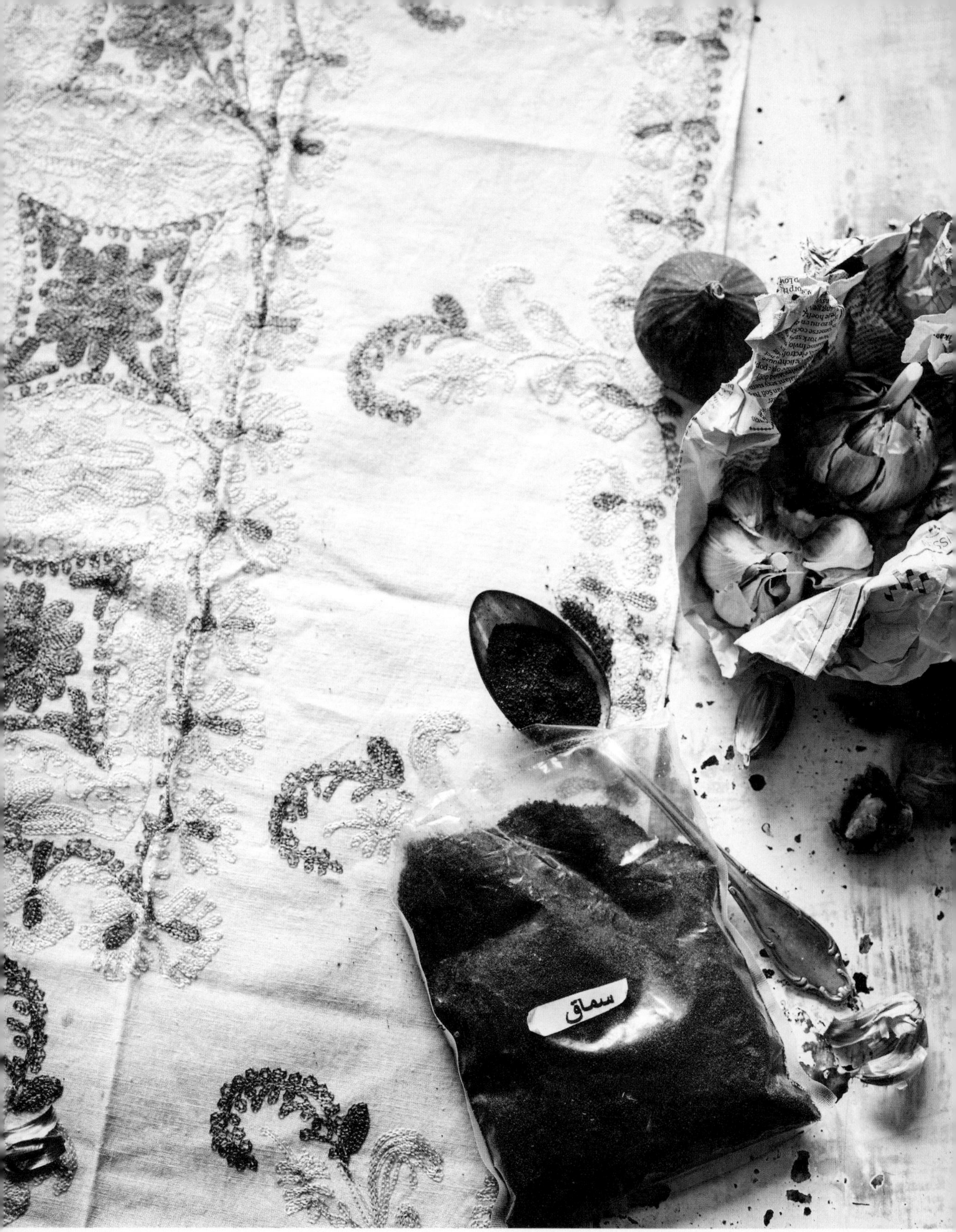
سماق

Essential seasonings you will need

Any Syrian dish can be prepared using the ingredients you would find in my kitchen cupboard, which are listed here for you. Thanks to ethnic specialty food stores, Middle Eastern stores, and well-stocked supermarkets, you are likely to find them available. Every city, and almost every town, has a small ethnic grocery nowadays and if that store doesn't have what I'm looking for, then I order it online.

SPICES
—

Sumac

(*Rhus coriaria*) There is a reason that my book is named for this spice and that it heads this list of basic ingredients. Its citrusy taste is both unmistakably Middle Eastern and mild. Sumac is the dried and ground fruit of the shrub bearing the same name. I use it in meat dishes and salads, as well as on fish. It is one of the primary ingredients in za'atar (see page 18).

7 Spices Blend

I discovered this spice mixture while studying in Beirut, Lebanon, where I lived above a coffee and spice roaster. I woke up to smells and morning sunlight streaming in through the window blinds, filling my room with their wafting presence.

In Syria, it is a perfumer—an a'atar—who mixes the 7 spices into a powered blend according to that a'atar's personal recipe. I like to use the 7 spices blend in rice pilafs or dishes that use ground beef. You can make my version of the 7 spices blend by combining: 2 tablespoons of ground black pepper, ¾ teaspoon of ground cloves, ½ tablespoon of ground coriander seeds, ½ tablespoon of ground nutmeg, ½ tablespoon of ground cardamom, and ½ tablespoon of ground cinnamon. If you like, you could also add ½ tablespoon of ground ginger.

Aleppo Pepper

(*Pepper annuum*) This pepper, also known as the Halaby pepper, is picked when it turns red and is then coarsely ground. The chili pepper flakes are sold as pul biber in Turkish markets. Thanks to the merchants of centuries past that traded along the Silk Road, the pepper spread from Aleppo to the whole world. The chili powder is not particularly hot, but is rather both bitter and sweet. I sometimes replace it with a mixture of 1 teaspoon of cayenne pepper and 2 teaspoons of sweet paprika.

A'atryaat

A'atryaat is a Syrian bouquet garni consisting of cinnamon sticks, bay leaves, cloves, and cardamom pods. The word a'atryaat means "perfume" and it is used to impart a subtle flavor to stews. The components of the bouquet garni are sometimes added directly to the pan, without bundling them first. A'atryaat garni is not sold pre-made; it is something you make yourself. My recipe uses: 2 cinnamon sticks, 2 cloves, 3 green cardamom pods, and 1 laurel leaf.

Pomegranate Molasses

This is my favorite ingredient! I always have a reserve of several bottles in my cupboard to give as gifts. Pomegranate molasses is made by cooking pomegranate juice until it is reduced down to a dark, thick, and sour syrup. I use it for salads, on meat, and in stews. You can buy pomegranate molasses in Middle Eastern and Turkish supermarkets, but buyer beware: some brands are very sweet—too sweet for my taste.

Dibs Al-Fleifleh

This red pepper paste comes in mild and spicy versions, and is an essential ingredient in muhammara (see page 83). It is very time-intensive to make it yourself, so I recommend going to a Turkish or Middle Eastern supermarket to buy it.

Tahini

Tahini's earthy and nutty flavor is emblematic of Middle Eastern cuisine. Syrians love to add it to anything, including desserts. I make tahini myself—you only need sesame seeds and olive oil. The advantage of homemade tahini is that you can toast the sesame seeds as much as you like and that you can choose your favorite oil. To make tahini, toast ¾ cup (100 g) of sesame seeds in a dry pan until they are a golden brown. Grind them in a food processor to form a thick paste. Moisten the sesame seed paste by very gradually adding 1 tablespoon of olive oil. It will keep in an airtight container or jar for a few months in the refrigerator.

Dried Mint

In Syria, people usually dry and grind their own mint. My mother would put the fresh mint leaves on a towel and set them out to dry for 2 or 3 days. Dried mint is used in dishes with yogurt or tomato, as well as in salads.

Za'atar

Za'atar means "thyme," but in practice the word always refers to a mix in which dried thyme is one of the star ingredients. There are two known variants of za'atar. The first is the "green" version, which is originally from Palestine. For one portion of this type of za'atar, I mix 5 tablespoons of dried thyme with 4 tablespoons of toasted sesame seeds, 1 tablespoon of sumac, and 1 tablespoon of marjoram.

The second version of za'atar is from Aleppo, and is a mix of 11 ingredients, including: fennel seeds, anise seeds, coriander seeds, watermelon seeds, dried and ground pomegranate seeds, and ground peanuts. It is a bit harder to make than Palestinian za'atar.

The mixes are not immune to change and versions may vary.

Nigella Seeds

(*Nigella sativa*) In Arabic, nigella seeds are called habet el baraka, which literally means "blessed seeds," referring to the well-known and lesser-known health benefits that these small blacks seeds may possess. You can find them in Turkish or Middle Eastern supermarkets or in better-stocked supermarkets. I use them in cheese dishes, soups, sambusak (page 71), and labneh (page 41).

Vermicelli

(*Sh'arieh*) This typically Italian ingredient is used in Syria as a particular addition to rice. We crumble the vermicelli and toast it before cooking it with rice. Since Syrians eat rice five or six times a week, that means we also eat a lot of vermicelli! My father didn't like it, so my mother would make her rice without vermicelli. My grandmother made vermicelli rice, though, and when we were growing up, my sisters and I always looked forward to her rice dishes.

Rose Water and Orange Blossom Water

This is perfumed water made by steam-distilling rose petals or orange blossom leaves. The steam condenses into water, which is then collected and bottled. Small quantities of either rose water or orange blossom water is used in atter (see below). The atter is then used as an ingredient in desserts.

Atter

Atter is a sugar syrup that forms the base for almost any Syrian dessert. You make it by warming 1 cup (250 ml) of water and stirring in 2⅓ cups (440 g) of sugar in a pan. As soon as the sugar is dissolved and the syrup starts to boil, you add 1 tablespoon of rose water or orange blossom water, as well a bit of grated lemon or orange peel and a bit of lemon or orange juice. Let it cool and store it in an airtight container. I usually prefer orange blossom water in my atter.

SAUCES

——

Serve the sauces immediately or store them refrigerated in sealed, airtight containers. The sauces will keep for one week.

Olive Oil, Lemon, Garlic Sauce

3½ tablespoons extra-virgin olive oil
Juice of 1 organic lemon
2 garlic cloves (pressed)
Salt

MY MOTHER'S SECRET INGREDIENT
½ teaspoon of red pepper paste (optional)

Whisk together all the ingredients and serve immediately.

———

This sauce is as versatile as it is simple. In Syria, it is used for straightforward dishes such as grilled fish, grilled chicken, fried cauliflower, or grilled eggplants, to name just a few.

Zhoug
Hot Green Chili Sauce

1 large bunch of cilantro
2 green rawit peppers (piri-piri, bird's eye, Thai chili)
3 green Anaheim peppers
2 garlic cloves (peeled)
¼ teaspoon of ground coriander
¼ teaspoon of ground cumin
4 tablespoons of extra-virgin olive oil
2 tablespoons of white wine vinegar
Salt (optional)
—
Blender

In a blender, combine all of the ingredients except for the olive oil, vinegar, and salt, and pulse until blended to a chunky consistency. Then add the olive oil and vinegar. Blend into a bright-green sauce. Taste and add salt if desired.

———

You can make a milder zhoug by substituting the rawit peppers with a milder chili variety.

Parsley–Cilantro Pesto

1 garlic clove (peeled)

Salt

1 bunch of cilantro (coarsely chopped)

1 bunch of flat-leaf parsley (coarsely chopped)

1 red chili pepper (coarsely chopped)

1 teaspoon of paprika

⅓ cup (50 g) of pine nuts (toasted)

2½ tablespoons of extra-virgin olive oil

Juice of ½ organic lemon

—

Food processor or mortar and pestle

Chop the garlic with a pinch of salt in a food processor or, even better, mash it with a mortar and pestle. Add the chopped cilantro, parsley, red chili pepper, and paprika. Mash or blend until smooth. Add the toasted pine nuts and grind them with the other ingredients until thick and smooth in consistency.

Drizzle the olive oil and lemon juice into the mixture and keep blending it until it has the consistency of a smooth pesto. Taste and add extra salt or lemon juice as desired.

Tarator
Tahini Sauce

3–4 tablespoons of tahini

Juice of 1 organic lemon

1 garlic clove (pressed)

3½ tablespoons water

Salt and pepper

2 sprigs of flat-leaf parsley (choppped)

Mix the tahini, lemon juice, and garlic with water in a small bowl until it is smooth and creamy. Add salt and pepper to taste and garnish with chopped parsley.

Green Tarator
Tahini–Mint Pesto

4 tablespoons of tahini

5 tablespoons of water

½ teaspoon of dried mint

¼ cup (15 g) of fresh mint leaves

Juice of 1 organic lemon

1 tablespoon of white vinegar

2 tablespoons of extra-virgin olive oil

1 garlic clove (peeled)

Salt

—

Blender

Blend all ingredients in a blender until everything is equally puréed. I think green tarator tastes better when it is somewhat thin in consistency. You could make it thicker by adding less water.

BREAKFAST

When I was young, all of us—children, grandchildren, brothers, sisters, nieces, and nephews—would go to my grandmother's house in Homs every weekend.

Weekend breakfast in my grandmother's garden

—

When I was young, all of us—children, grandchildren, brothers, sisters, nieces, and nephews—would go to my grandmother's house in Homs every weekend. Her house was just on the outskirts of the city, and in her garden, hidden away among the fruit trees, there was a long table with a flower tablecloth. We would sit at that table on chairs, stools, or boxes turned upside down. Sometimes we even sat on an old swing. And we would eat. This is where the lives and stories of all the family members intertwined. It was where we came together again after a week of work or school, or during the lazy vacation days.

We ate and talked—each was just as important as the other. As a child, it never occurred to me that these get-togethers would ever not happen. Of course we ended up at grandmother's house on Friday morning. Of course we drank coffee and tea. Of course the table was full of delicious food: from everyday hawadir—breakfast dishes like labneh, za'atar, jam, and soft cheese—to weekend treats like musabaha (see page 26) and foul mudammas (see page 33). We would only stop eating when our tummies were stuffed. And of course we would start another round of wonderful eating a little while later.

Although women are the ones who cook in the traditional Syrian kitchen, the preparation of hummus and bean dishes (typically found in a weekend spread) is a man's task. While the children played, the men—my grandfather, my father, or an uncle—would fulfill their Friday morning responsibilities. My father's specialty was foul mudammas, fava beans in olive oil. He, alone, was able to achieve the perfect balance of garlic and lemon.

Since those days, it has become impossible to even imagine holding those carefree weekend breakfasts in my grandmother's garden. The war in Syria has devastated Homs, as it has many other places. My family is scattered throughout the world. Even if we wanted to, the days when all thirty (or more) of us gathered at the table to chat for hours on end, reaching over to pick a grape from the vine or to pluck a peach from the tree, are, unfortunately, long gone. We do, when and where we can, come together for smaller family reunions. At those times, we sit once more at the breakfast table and make the best of it.

Musabaha
— Chickpeas in Yogurt–Tahini Sauce

In a small pan, combine the chickpeas in their liquid, 2 cups (500 ml) of water, and the baking soda. Boil for approximately 30 minutes until very soft.

In a bowl, combine the yogurt, tahini, garlic, and lemon juice and add salt to taste. The tahini is the only thing you need to thicken the sauce.

Drain the cooked chickpeas over a bowl to catch the liquid, and set the liquid aside. Using a fork, mash half of the chickpeas with the reserved cooking liquid and then mix in the yogurt sauce. The warm cooking liquid will make the yogurt–tahini sauce amazingly creamy. Stir the rest of the chickpeas into the sauce.

Spoon the sauce into a dish and sprinkle it with ground cumin and paprika. Garnish with toasted cashews and pine nuts and drizzle some extra-virgin olive oil on top.

SERVES 4

28 oz (800 g) can of chickpeas
¾ teaspoon of baking soda
2 tablespoons of Greek yogurt
6 tablespoons of tahini
3 garlic cloves (pressed)
Juice of 1 organic lemon
Salt

TO SERVE
1 teaspoon of ground cumin
1 teaspoon of paprika
3 tablespoons of cashew nuts (toasted)
3 tablespoons of pine nuts (toasted)
Extra-virgin olive oil

Jazmaz
— Eggs in Tomato Sauce with Chilies

PREPARATION

Heat the olive oil in a large nonstick frying pan set over medium heat and sauté the onion in the hot oil for 5 minutes, or until it starts to brown. Add the garlic and sauté it with the onion for another couple of minutes, stirring so that the garlic doesn't burn.

Stir in the chili, diced tomatoes (along with the juice), and paprika. Add salt and pepper to taste. Turn the heat to low and simmer the sauce for 5 minutes, or until it thickens and reduces a bit.

With a spoon, make four little wells in the sauce and crack an egg into each so that the sauce surrounds each one. Cover and cook for 5 to 6 minutes, plus an extra 2 minutes if the yolks need to cook thoroughly.

Serve in the frying pan, garnished with chopped parsley and olive slices. Add salt and pepper to taste. This is delicious eaten with warm bread.

INGREDIENTS

SERVES 4

2 tablespoons of extra-virgin olive oil
1 onion (chopped)
2 garlic cloves (pressed)
1 hot chili pepper (halved lengthwise)
3 medium tomatoes (diced, juices retained)
1 teaspoon of paprika
Salt and pepper
4 eggs
1 handful of flat-leaf parsley (coarsely chopped)
1 handful of black olives (pitted and sliced)

Jazmaz, as it is known in Syria, is also popular in Levantine cuisine, where it goes by the name shakshoka. It is a simple dish that could be served at any time of the day—breakfast, brunch, lunch, or dinner. Every family makes it a little bit differently. The differences are small, but important: a little bit of extra chili pepper, eggs that range from softly cooked to completely hard-boiled. I like my jazmaz spicy and I eat it the traditional way, with flatbread or, in a modern twist, with baguette.

Man'oushe za'atar
— Za'atar Flatbread

PREPARATION

DOUGH—FIRST STEP

In a large bowl, mix the yeast with the sugar. Whisk in the warm water until the yeast and sugar have dissolved. Gradually add the flour and mix until completely incorporated, with no visible lumps in the dough. Cover the bowl with a tea towel and set aside to rise for 15 minutes.

For the topping, mix the za'atar and olive oil in a small dish and set aside.

Preheat the oven to 480°F (250°C). Lightly flour a baking sheet.

DOUGH—SECOND STEP

Add the yogurt, oil, flour, and salt to the dough. Knead it by hand for 7–10 minutes, until smooth, soft, and elastic. Add some extra flour to the dough if it sticks to your hands. Divide the dough into four balls and place them on the floured sheet. Cover with a tea towel to keep the dough from drying out.

Dust your work surface lightly with flour. Take a ball of dough and flatten it with the palm of your hand. Roll it out with a floured rolling pin and shape it into an oval that measures 14 x 8 inches (35 x 20 cm) across, and ⅛–¼ inch (3–5 mm) thick. Repeat with the other balls of dough.

Mix the za'atar topping and spread a thin layer over the rolled-out dough. Line a baking sheet with parchment paper. Place the man'oushe on the paper and bake them in the oven for 5–7 minutes, or until the edges are a golden brown.

———

Serve warm with labneh, cucumbers, tomatoes, pickles, and mint.

INGREDIENTS

MAKES 4

DOUGH—FIRST STEP
1 (7 g) envelope of instant yeast
2 teaspoons of sugar
Generous ¾ cup (200 ml) of warm water
1 cup (125 g) of all-purpose flour

DOUGH—SECOND STEP
¼ cup (75 g) of Greek yogurt
2 tablespoons of vegetable oil
2¼ cups (275 g) of all-purpose flour,
    plus extra for dusting
Salt

TOPPING
4 tablespoons of za'atar (see page 18),
    plus extra if needed
4 tablespoons of extra-virgin olive oil,
    plus extra if needed

Flatbread is very popular in Syria. It can be thick or thin, and can be prepared with one of many toppings. This version with za'atar (a mix of thyme and sesame seeds) and olive oil is sold everywhere and is a popular street food.

When I was a student, this is the flatbread I would buy on my way to the college—a breakfast on-the-go, rolled up and filled with cucumber, tomato, pickles, and mint. Now, ten years later, the little shop where I always bought it is still there. To my surprise, the owner still recognized me after all these years. That says something about how often I would swing by . . .

Foul mudammas
— Fava Beans in Olive Oil

In a small pan, boil the fava beans in 1¼ cups (300 ml) of water over medium heat for 7 minutes.

Then place half of the cooked fava beans and a scant ½ cup (100 ml) of the cooking water into a bowl, along with the olive oil, lemon juice, garlic, and cumin. Coarsely mash the ingredients together and add salt and pepper to taste. Gently mix in the rest of the cooked fava beans. Arrange the tomato pieces on top, sprinkle with chopped parsley, and liberally drizzle the dish with olive oil.

Serve with warm bread to mop up the tasty juices.

―――――

*If you would prefer to use dried fava beans, soak them first in water overnight and cook them for about 1 hour in fresh water.

INGREDIENTS

SERVES 4

28 oz (800 g) can of fava beans (drained and rinsed)*
3½ tablespoons of extra-virgin olive oil
Juice of 1 organic lemon
2 garlic cloves (pressed)
¼ teaspoon of ground cumin
Salt and pepper

TOPPINGS
1 tomato (diced)
1 bunch of flat-leaf parsley
  (coarsely chopped)
Extra-virgin olive oil

Seeing foul mudammas on the breakfast table always gave me a happy feeling: the weekend has started! Dried fava beans, which are typical for this dish, must first be soaked, drained, and then cooked— a time-intensive task. Luckily, canned fava beans are readily available nowadays, and they're quite a bit faster and easier to prepare. Foul mudammas is eaten with a spoon in one hand and a piece of flatbread in the other to mop up all the delicious olive oil.

Murabba el-batinjan
— Eggplant Jam

PREPARATION

In a large bowl, dissolve the calcium hydroxide powder in the warm water. Stir for one minute, then set aside for 30 minutes.

Any undissolved powder will sink to the bottom. Pour the water into another bowl and throw away any undissolved powder.

Set the peeled eggplants into the calcium hydroxide solution. Set a plate on top of the bowl to keep them submerged. Soak the eggplants in this way for 24 hours.

When the 24 hours have passed, drain and rinse the eggplants to rid them of any remaining calcium hydroxide. Soak them in clean tap water for another 15 minutes. Drain.

Place the eggplants in a large pan and then fill with warm water until the water just barely covers the eggplants. Cook them gently on medium heat for 30 minutes. They should be soft but not mushy. Remove the eggplants from the water and let them cool until you can handle them with your hands. Press the eggplants between your palms and gently use your fingers to squeeze out any extra moisture.

To make the syrup, dissolve the sugar in the water in a deep pot. Set the dissolved sugar on high heat, changing it to low heat as soon as the syrup starts to boil. Add the eggplants and cinnamon sticks, stirring occasionally. Simmer the jam for 1 hour.

Add the citric acid to the pot and keep simmering for another 15 minutes. The eggplants should be somewhat transparent and light-brown in color. Set them aside to cool completely.

INGREDIENTS

MAKES 2 PINT-SIZE JARS (16 OZ / 500 ML EACH)

7 oz (200 g) of food-grade calcium hydroxide powder (pickling lime, or slaked lime, optional)
12½ cups (3 liters) of warm water
2 lb 4 oz (1 kg) of baby eggplants (thoroughly cleaned, peeled, stems removed)

FOR THE SYRUP
2 lb 4 oz (1 kg) of sugar
4¼ cups (1 liter) water
2 cinnamon sticks
¼ teaspoon of citric acid

TO SERVE
1 handful of walnuts (coarsely chopped)

Syrians adore eggplants. They love them so much that they even make sweet things with eggplants, like this jam. Eat it on bread with butter, or with some walnuts crumbled on top. Although that may sound like a strange way to eat eggplant, I encourage you to try this recipe. Even my sister (the only Syrian I know who isn't an eggplant-lover) eats it with relish!

Spoon the cooled eggplants equally into the two jars. Add a bit of the syrup to each. Cover the jars and store in the refrigerator. Serve the jam with coarsely chopped walnuts sprinkled on top.

BREAKFAST

Ejjeh
— Egg Pancakes with Parsley

PREPARATION

Crack the eggs into a large bowl. Beat in the flour, ground coriander, and paprika until there are no lumps visible.

Purée the onion in a food processor. Spoon the onion purée into a fine sieve and press with the curved part of a spoon to squeeze the moisture out. Then add the onion purée to the egg mixture. Set aside some of the parsley and scallion to use as a garnish, and add the rest to the egg batter. Add salt and pepper to taste.

Heat some butter in a saucepan until it starts to foam. Add 2 spoonfuls of the batter to the pan and use the back side of the spoon to form a pancake of approximately 6 inches (15 cm) in diameter. Cook the pancake for 2–3 minutes on each side, or until golden brown. Repeat until all the batter has been used—you should have about 6.

Sprinkle the reserved chopped scallion and parsley over the pancakes and serve.

INGREDIENTS

SERVES 6

6 eggs
2 tablespoons of all-purpose flour
2 teaspoons of ground coriander
2 teaspoons of mild paprika
1 white onion (quartered)
1 bunch of flat-leaf parsley (finely chopped)
1 scallion (chopped)
Salt and pepper
Butter for frying
—
Food processor

Ejjeh is reminiscent of an Italian frittata and is a bit of a hodge-podge: beaten egg with vegetables mixed in, fried in the shape of a pancake. My sister and I used to eat ejjeh as a sandwich rolled up with slices of turkey and lettuce, or with feta cheese, cucumber, and olives. Good for breakfast, brunch, or lunch.

Khebzeh harra
— Flatbread with Spicy Tomato Sauce

PREPARATION

Preheat the oven to 480°F (250°C).

DOUGH—FIRST STEP
In a large bowl, mix the yeast with the sugar. Whisk in the warm water until the yeast and sugar have dissolved. Gradually add the flour and mix until completely incorporated, with no visible lumps in the dough. Cover the bowl with a tea towel and set aside to rise for 15 minutes.

DOUGH—SECOND STEP
Add the yogurt, oil, flour, and salt to the dough. Knead it by hand for 7–10 minutes, until smooth, soft, and elastic. Add some extra flour to the dough if it sticks to your hands.

Divide the dough into egg-sized balls. Set the balls of dough on a floured baking sheet and cover with a tea towel so the dough doesn't dry out.

In a separate bowl, combine all the ingredients for the tomato sauce. Add salt and pepper to taste.

Lightly flour the kneading surface. Use your palm to flatten each ball of dough. Roll them out with a floured rolling pin until they are 8 inches (20 cm) in diameter and ⅛–¼ inch (3–5 mm) thick.

Spread a couple of spoonfuls of the tomato sauce on top of the circles of rolled-out dough.

Line a baking sheet with parchment paper. Place the khebzeh harra on the parchment paper and, if desired, crack an egg over the middle of each one. Bake for 5–7 minutes, or until the edges are a golden brown. If you like, garnish the khebzeh harra with chopped parsley.

INGREDIENTS

SERVES 8

DOUGH—FIRST STEP
1 (7 g) envelope of instant yeast
2 teaspoons of sugar
Generous ¾ cup (200 ml) of warm water
1 cup (125 g) of all-purpose flour

DOUGH—SECOND STEP
¼ cup (75 g) of Greek yogurt
2 tablespoons of vegetable oil
2¼ cup (275 g) of all-purpose flour,
   plus extra for dusting
Salt

FOR THE TOMATO SAUCE
1 onion (chopped)
28 oz (800 g) can of whole tomatoes
   (chopped and then strained)
1 teaspoon of nigella seeds
1 tablespoon of anise seeds
2 teaspoons of red pepper paste
1 tablespoon of crushed red pepper flakes
2 teaspoons of extra-virgin olive oil
Salt and pepper

TOPPINGS
8 small eggs (optional)
1 handful of flat-leaf parsley
   (coarsely chopped) (optional)

Khebzeh harra literally means "spicy bread." Syrians usually buy it at a place called a ferran—a bakery that specializes in flatbreads topped with all sorts of tasty combinations. Man'oushe za'atar (see page 30) and sfeeha (see page 75) are also bought at a ferran, for example. Khebzeh harra is bread topped with a tasty mixture of tomato and red pepper paste. I add anise seed as a personal touch.

Labneh
— Yogurt Cheese

Mix together the yogurt and lemon juice, if using. Liberally add salt to taste (some of the salt will drain out with the moisture in the yogurt).

Line a fine sieve with a double layer of cheesecloth. You could also use a clean cotton tea towel. Set the sieve over a bowl to catch the drained liquid.

Spoon the yogurt into the lined sieve. Gather up the edges of the cloth or towel. Twist them to form a tight bundle and knot the ends. Refrigerate the yogurt bundle in the sieve (including the bowl to catch any liquid) for at least 12 hours. Afterwards the labneh should be the consistency of cream cheese. Spoon the labneh into a serving bowl, liberally drizzle with extra-virgin olive oil, and garnish with your toppings of choice.

INGREDIENTS

SERVES 6–8

1 lb 2 oz (500 g) of Greek yogurt
Juice of ½ organic lemon (optional)
Salt

TO SERVE
Good quality extra-virgin olive oil

TO GARNISH
Dried mint, Aleppo pepper, za'atar, oregano, dried thyme, nigella seeds, or sumac
—
Cheesecloth or clean cotton tea towel

Labneh is sold ready to eat in every supermarket in Syria. It's a bit more difficult to find elsewhere, but luckily it's still possible. Syrian labneh is fresher and has a more tangy taste than Western varieties of thickened yogurt, so you may wish to add some lemon juice like I do.

Labneh balls

The longer the labneh drains, the thicker it becomes. After draining it for 3 days it will be so thick that you will be able to form the cheese into small, roughly walnut-sized balls.

Arrange the labneh balls in a glass jar. Pour olive oil over the balls until they are covered completely, and store them in the refrigerator. Add a sprig of fresh thyme, a clove of garlic, a chili pepper, or all three if you would like to flavors the cheese.

To serve, roll the balls in a topping of your choice. Serve with bread or crackers.

INGREDIENTS

MAKES 15

1 quantity of labneh (page 41)
Extra-virgin olive oil (for storing)
Sprig of fresh thyme, 1 garlic clove,
  and/or 1 chili pepper

TO GARNISH
Dried mint, Aleppo pepper, za'atar, oregano,
  dried thyme, nigella seeds, or sumac

The yogurt cheese labneh is a mainstay of any Syrian breakfast spread. In my family, it is also often served as part of a light dinner: labneh with some paprika and dried mint sprinkled on top, accompanied by olives and cheese. Labneh was always in the refrigerator when I was growing up.

MEZZE
FOR SHARING AND SPREADING

The marble floors
of our house were
polished to gleaming,
there were bright
flowers wherever you
looked, and chairs
stood lined up against
the parlor walls.

My mother's annual soirées
"Women only"
—

I have childhood memories of my mother throwing two big parties a year. One was a dress-up affair, a dinner party for couples. The other was an extravagant evening, a glamorous soirée, for her women friends, who would come dressed in glittering gold and bright, sequined dresses. The marble floors of our house were polished to gleaming, there were bright flowers wherever you looked, and chairs stood lined up against the parlor walls. This was where my mother received her friends—sometimes up to seventy or eighty—each and every one of them dressed to the nines.

You heard the quiet murmur of women's conversation as guests arrived, and then: the buffet. Tables linked up in a row down the entire length of the parlor and out into the garden, laden with food and drink. The variety and number of offerings was dazzling: kibbeh, sayniyi, ouzi, muhammara, moutabal. . . Women took over the entire lower level and the garden to mingle, and then, after the eating was done, the music started. That was when I realized why all the chairs were pushed up against the walls. It was to make space for a dance floor, to put the parlor to good use!

I was mesmerized by this annual soirée. As a small boy, I would pretend that I was invisible and walk around during the festivities, weaving in and out among the guests. It was like diving into a whole different world. When I turned ten years old, I was banished upstairs. So I would watch, transfixed, from a perch on the staircase. As part of the close-knit Syrian community in Jeddah, Saudi Arabia, where we lived in those days, I was used to seeing women wearing black abajas outside the house, in accordance with the strict rules that were in effect. But the women I saw at mother's parties were relaxed. They laughed, they danced. It was another reality altogether. Syrian culture, so much more free than that of many other Middle Eastern countries, came to life before my eyes.

And my father? He was kicked out of the house for the evening. I suppose he might very well have held his own fête, meeting up with numerous buddies somewhere else in the neighborhood . . .

The house that hosted those evenings has long since been demolished. The women guests now live scattered throughout the world. And, while it's true that my mother has always had a talent for forming friendships no matter where she's lived, and even though she's always had a large social circle, the "women only" soirées were special in their uniqueness.

Moutabal
— Roasted Eggplant, Yogurt, and Tahini Dip

PREPARATION

Roast the eggplant over an open flame, gas burner, or grill, turning occasionally, for about 20 minutes, until the skin is charred and the flesh is soft. Alternatively, you can roast the eggplant for about 40 minutes in an oven preheated to 480°F (250°C). Set aside to cool.

When the eggplant is cool enough to handle, scrape out the flesh, discarding the skin, and either mash it with a fork or purée it in a food processor. Add the tahini, yogurt, garlic, and lemon juice to the mashed eggplant and blend well. Add salt to taste.

Spoon the dip into a bowl and drizzle with some extra-virgin olive oil. Garnish with pomegranate seeds.

———

Moutabal is usually served cold, as part of a mezze spread, though I harbor a secret preference for the more pronounced flavors of moutabal served warm.

INGREDIENTS

SERVES 4

1 eggplant
2 tablespoons of tahini
3 tablespoons of Greek yogurt
2 garlic cloves (pressed)
Juice of 1 organic lemon
Salt

TO SERVE
Extra-virgin olive oil
1 handful of pomegranate seeds

My grandmother had an outdoor kitchen in her garden, set up at a safe distance to keep smells out of the house. We called this kitchen the "eggplant oven." This is where the eggplants were either roasted over an open fire or fried, though any smelly kitchen task, actually, was moved outside to the eggplant oven. So take heed! You'll have to put up with some strong smells before eventually enjoying the sultry, smoky taste of this dip.

Batersh
— Roasted Eggplant Dip with Tomato–Meat Sauce

PREPARATION

Heat the oil in a saucepan and fry the onion with the garlic for 4–5 minutes, or until they begin to soften.

Add the ground beef and brown for 5 minutes, breaking it into small pieces, until completely cooked. Add the diced tomatoes, and salt and pepper to taste. Simmer the sauce on low heat for 10 minutes.

Spoon the moutabal into a bowl and top with the tomato and beef sauce. Garnish with parsley and toasted pine nuts.

INGREDIENTS

SERVES 4

1 recipe of moutabal (page 48)
2 tablespoons of extra-virgin olive oil
1 small onion (chopped)
1 garlic clove (minced)
5½ oz (150 g) of ground beef
7 oz (200 g) of canned diced tomatoes
Salt and pepper

TO SERVE
1 handful of flat-leaf parsley (chopped)
3 tablespoons of pine nuts (toasted)

Batersh is a special combination of moutabal (page 48) and a tomato and ground beef sauce. This may sound like a strange pairing, but it tastes amazing. It is a specialty from the city of Hama and you'd be hard-pressed to have it served to you outside of the city's walls—unless you were to eat with my family! Ever since we discovered this dish during a family trip, it has been a staple in my mother's repertoire. We eat it as a warm appetizer, or as a light dinner with flatbread. Or sometimes simply as it is, without anything else. Highly recommended!

Mufarakeh
— Eggs with Beef and Zucchini

Heat the oil in a large pan. Add the onion and the zucchini and fry, stirring, until golden brown.

Add the ground beef and cook, breaking it up into small pieces with a wooden spoon, until browned and completely cooked, 5 minutes. Add salt and pepper to taste.

Turn the heat to low and make four little wells in the beef mixture. Crack an egg into each well. Cover and cook for 3–5 minutes, or until the yolks are thoroughly cooked.

Serve in the pan, generously sprinkled with parsley.

INGREDIENTS

SERVES 4

2 tablespoons of extra-virgin olive oil
1 onion (chopped)
1 zucchini (cut into large pieces)
9 oz (250 g) of ground beef
Salt and pepper
4 eggs
1 bunch of flat-leaf parsley (coarsely chopped)

This dish reminds me of long days out and about with my family when we lived in Saudi Arabia—hours of shopping at Ikea, for example (yes, Ikea is everywhere). When we got back home, my mother would make something simple and tasty with whatever we had on hand. We always ate it with flatbread—something I still do to this day.

Eggplant and red pepper dip

Preheat the oven to 425°F (220°C).

Spread the eggplant pieces on a baking sheet, toss them in 2 tablespoons of the olive oil, and salt liberally. Bake the eggplant for 25 minutes, until golden brown and soft. Cool.

Blend the cooled eggplant in a food processor, along with the roasted red peppers, garlic, cayenne pepper, lemon juice, vinegar, and the remaning 1 tablespoon of olive oil. Pulse until smooth and creamy. Taste and add salt and pepper as desired. Pulse one more time.

Spoon the dip into a dish, cover, and refrigerate for 2 hours to give time for the flavors to develop. Serve the dip cold, with flatbread or crackers.

INGREDIENTS

SERVES 6

2 eggplants (peeled, stems removed, cut into pieces)
3 tablespoons of extra-virgin olive oil
Sea salt
12 oz (350 g) jar of roasted red peppers (drained)
2 garlic cloves (peeled)
1 teaspoon of cayenne pepper
Juice of 1 organic lemon
2 teaspoons of white vinegar
Salt and pepper
—
Food processor

You won't readily find this dip in Syria—it is one of my own creations. In my attempts to find even more recipes with eggplant as the star ingredient, I tried combining it with muhammara (see page 83). This delicious dip is the result: it is creamy thanks to the eggplant, and a touch spicy due to the cayenne pepper. It is wonderful when served with kibbeh (see page 156).

Batata harra
— Spicy Potatoes with Garlic and Cilantro

PREPARATION

Preheat the oven to 450°F (230°C).

Bring a large pot of water to a boil. Add the potatoes to the boiling water and cook for 7 minutes. Drain the partially cooked potatoes, return them to the pot, cover, and steam them in their own heat for a few minutes.

Line a baking sheet with parchment paper. Spread the potatoes across the pan and rub them with 3½ tablespoons of the olive oil, and the red pepper paste, paprika, and sea salt. Roast for 15–20 minutes, turning them a few times, until golden brown and just tender.

Remove the potatoes from the oven. Toss with garlic, lemon juice, and the chopped cilantro (reserving some to garnish) until evenly covered, and then continue to roast for another 5 minutes.

To serve, drizzle the remaining 3½ tablespoons of the extra-virgin olive oil over the batata harra and sprinkle with the reserved chopped cilantro.

INGREDIENTS

SERVES 4

2 lb 4 oz (1 kg) of boiling
  potatoes with skin (6 medium),
  (cut into 2 inch/5 cm pieces)
Scant ½ cup (100 ml) of extra-virgin olive oil
2 tablespoons of spicy red pepper paste
1 teaspoon of paprika
Sea salt
4 garlic cloves (pressed)
Juice of 1 organic lemon
1 large bunch of cilantro
  (coarsely chopped)

The potato has not played as much of an important role in traditional Syrian cuisine as it has in Western food. Syrian go-to carbohydrates are traditionally bulgur, rice, and bread. And yet, French fries can frequently be found on the mezze table, especially in restaurants. Make these spicy potatoes instead—you'll never miss the fries.

Hummus

Hummus is the king of the Syrian table. Many
countries are convinced that they are the inventors
of this dip. And I don't want to debate this point too
finely, but I will just say that I'm from Homs and
hummus just happens to be spelled exactly the same
way in Arabic: homs. So, who knows? Let's call it
an international food. I'm happy as long as everyone
enjoys it.

Two types of hummus are common in Syria: one
with tahini and one with olive oil. Hummus with
olive oil is somewhat coarser in texture and not quite
as creamy as the tahini hummus. You can definitely
taste the olive oil, so use the best quality you can
find. Both types of hummus can be served with
toppings. My favorite toppings are small cubes of
lamb fried in olive oil, pine nuts toasted in olive oil,
and fried pieces of merguez sausage that you can
make by removing the meat from the casing.

Hummus bi tahini
— Hummus with Tahini

PREPARATION

Bring a small saucepan of water to a boil. Add the chickpeas and baking soda. Boil for 30 minutes, or until very soft, making sure the chickpeas are covered with water the entire time (add extra water if needed). Remove the pan from the heat. Set aside to cool the chickpeas in the cooking liquid. Once cool, drain the chickpeas, reserving the liquid.

Place the chickpeas and 7 tablespoons of the cooking liquid into a food processor. Add the garlic, lemon juice, tahini, olive oil, and salt and blend. Taste and add more salt as desired. Continue blending the hummus until it is very smooth and creamy (about 2 minutes). Add 1–2 tablespoons more cooking liquid, if needed, to achieve this consistency.

Hummus is invariably served in a wide, shallow dish. Drizzle liberally with extra-virgin olive oil, and garnish with chopped parsley and a pinch of paprika.

———

*If you choose to use dried chickpeas, soak ¾ cup (125 g) dried chickpeas in plenty of water overnight. Discard the soaking water and simmer the chickpeas in fresh water and the baking soda until they are very soft (this can take anywhere from 1 to 3 hours, depending on the size and age of your chickpeas).

INGREDIENTS

SERVES 3–4

14 oz (400 g) can of chickpeas (drained and rinsed)*
¾ teaspoon of baking soda
1 garlic clove (pressed)
3 tablespoons of freshly squeezed lemon juice
3 tablespoons of tahini
4 tablespoons of extra-virgin olive oil
Salt

TO SERVE
Extra-virgin olive oil
1 handful of flat-leaf parsley (chopped)
Pinch of paprika
—
Food processor

Hummus bi zeit
— Hummus with Olive Oil

Bring a small saucepan of water to a boil. Add the chickpeas and baking soda. Boil for 30 minutes, or until very soft, making sure the chickpeas are covered with water the entire time (add extra water if needed). Remove the pan from the heat. Set aside to cool the chickpeas in the cooking liquid. You will use this liquid later.

Reserve a handful of the cooked chickpeas to garnish. Once cooled, transfer the rest of the chickpeas and 1–2 tablespoons of the cooking liquid to your food processor. Add the garlic, olive oil, cumin, and 1 teaspoon of salt. Pulse a few times, then taste and add more salt as desired. Continue blending the hummus for another minute or so. The consistency and texture of hummus bi zeit should be thick and not completely smooth.

Always serve hummus in a wide, shallow dish. Drizzle liberally with olive oil. Garnish the hummus with the reserved chickpeas, and the paprika and cumin.

——

Fried cubes of lamb, toasted pine nuts, or both are toppings that complement the hummus well.

It is also delicious with spicy merguez sausages— these aren't Syrian, but they do add wonderful flavors!

SERVES 3–4

14 oz (400 g) can of chickpeas
   (drained and rinsed)
¾ teaspoon of baking soda
1 garlic clove (pressed)
4 tablespoons of extra-virgin olive oil
½ teaspoon of ground cumin
Salt

TO SERVE
Extra-virgin olive oil
Pinch of paprika
Pinch of ground cumin
—
Food processor

Foul ma'ala
— Fresh Fava Beans with Cilantro and Garlic

PREPARATION

In a large saucepan, heat the oil over medium heat.
Fry the garlic until golden brown, being careful
not to let it burn. Stir in the cilantro and fry for
1 minute.

Add the beans to the saucepan and fry everything
together for 5 minutes, or until the beans are fully
cooked. Season with salt and pepper to taste.

Squeeze some lemon juice over the beans and
drizzle liberally with extra-virgin olive oil.
Serve with flatbread.

INGREDIENTS

SERVES 4

4 tablespoons of extra-virgin olive oil
4 garlic cloves (pressed)
1 bunch of cilantro
  (coarsely chopped)
1 lb 12 oz (800 g) podded fresh or frozen fava beans
  (peeled if desired)
Salt and pepper
Juice of 1 organic lemon
Extra-virgin olive oil

TO SERVE
Flatbread

*This was one of my father's favorite dishes—he loved
to dip his flatbread into it. (To be honest, he dipped his
flatbread into anything!) He loved how the pure taste
of the simple ingredients came through in every bite.
This recipe really lets those ingredients shine. This dish
confirms what I learned from him: not everything has
to be complicated.*

Moutabal shawandar
— Beet and Tahini Dip

PREPARATION

Chop the beets into chunks and put them in a food processor. Add the yogurt, garlic, tahini, lemon juice, salt, and pepper. Process on the pulse setting until well mixed, but not too finely puréed. I like this dip with a little texture.

Serve in a dish, drizzled with extra-virgin olive oil, and garnished with nigella seeds. I sometimes sprinkle on some chopped parsley too.

INGREDIENTS

SERVES 4

**1 lb 2 oz (500 g) of cooked beets
(drained, if you use vacuum-packed)**
½ cup (125 g) of Greek yogurt
2 garlic cloves (peeled)
2 tablespoons of tahini
Juice of 1 organic lemon
Salt and pepper

TO SERVE
Extra-virgin olive oil
1 teaspoon of nigella seeds
**Handful of chopped flat-leaf parsley
(optional)**
—
Food processor

This dip has an invitingly bright color. It is actually a moutabal (see page 48), but made with red beets instead of eggplants. You won't commonly find it in the Middle East, but it has achieved a somewhat mythical status in my family (my mother is crazy about beets). Their festive sweetness, combined with the sour yogurt and earthy tahini, delights the palate. I eat it with kibbeh sayniyi (see page 163), or with flatbread or crackers.

Fatayer bi sabankh
— Spinach Pies

FIRST, MAKE THE FILLING

Bring a large pot of water to a boil. Add the
spinach, cover, and immediately turn the heat off.
The spinach will cook in the hot water. Let it cool in
the cooking water, then drain the spinach using a
strainer, pressing to squeeze out all the water.

In a nonstick pan, heat 2 tablespoons of oil over
medium heat. Fry the onion for 3 minutes. Add
the strained spinach, crushed red pepper flakes,
sumac, and pomegranate molasses, and fry for
another 5 minutes and until all the moisture has
evaporated. Turn off the heat and drizzle the mixture
with the remaining tablespoon of olive oil and the
lemon juice. Add salt and pepper to taste. Cool.

Preheat the oven to 425°F (220°C).

DOUGH—FIRST STEP

In a large bowl, mix the yeast with the sugar. Whisk
in the warm water until the yeast and sugar have
dissolved. Gradually add the flour and mix until
completely incorporated, with no visible lumps in the
dough. Cover the bowl with a tea towel and set aside
to rise for 15 minutes.

DOUGH—SECOND STEP

Add the yogurt, oil, flour, and salt to the dough.
Knead it by hand for 7–10 minutes, until smooth,
soft, and elastic. Add some extra flour to the dough if
it sticks to your hands.

Sprinkle your work surface with flour. Form the
dough into 25–30 balls, each about the size of an
egg. Roll the balls of dough into circles measuring
4 inches (10 cm) in diameter.

INGREDIENTS

MAKES 25–30

FOR THE FILLING
1 lb 2 oz (500 g) of baby spinach
3 tablespoons of extra-virgin olive oil,
   plus extra for brushing
1 large onion (coarsely chopped)
1 tablespoon of crushed red pepper flakes
2 teaspoons of sumac
2 tablespoons of pomegranate molasses
Juice of 1 organic lemon
Salt and pepper

DOUGH—FIRST STEP
1 envelope (7 g) of instant yeast
2 teaspoons of sugar
Generous ¾ cup (200 ml) of warm water
1 cup (125 g) of all-purpose flour

DOUGH—SECOND STEP
¼ cup (75 g) of Greek yogurt
2 tablespoons of vegetable oil
2¼ cups (275 g) of all-purpose flour,
   plus extra for dusting
1 teaspoon of salt

Place a tablespoon of filling in the middle of each
circle and form triangle shapes by folding the edges
towards the center. Press the seams together.

Line a baking sheet with parchment paper. Place the
filled triangles on the prepared sheet and brush with
olive oil. Bake for 15 minutes, or until golden brown
and crispy.

I'll let you in on a secret: if you see a filled pastry in the shape of a triangle, you can be sure that the filling contains spinach. The triangular shape goes hand in hand with spinach. For this fatayer bi sabankh, I dress up the spinach with pomegranate, lemon, and sumac. Spinach pies are perfect as a snack or as a lunch on the go.

Sambusak
— Filo Rolls with Cheese Filling

PREPARATION

In a bowl, mix together the mozzarella, feta, parsley, and nigella seeds.

Place a sheet of filo dough flat in front of you. Spoon a tablespoon of the cheese filling onto the sheet in 3-inch (8 cm) line, about 2 inches (5 cm) from the edge closest to you. Fold the edge over the filling and press the filo dough down with moistened fingers so that it sticks. Then fold the side edges towards the inside. Roll up the filled filo dough like a cigar to form the pastry roll. Seal the seams with a little bit of water. The roll should be about 3 inches (8 cm) long. Repeat using the rest of the filling and filo dough.

Preheat the oven to 400°F (200°C). Grease a baking sheet with olive oil.

Arrange the rolls on the prepared sheet, at least ¼ inch (5 mm) apart. Brush the filo rolls with olive oil. Bake for 15 minutes, turning them occasionally so that they crisp evenly. They should be golden brown on all sides.

INGREDIENTS

MAKES 12

⅔ cup (100 g) of mozzarella cheese (mashed)
⅓ cup (50 g) of crumbled feta cheese
1 small bunch of flat-leaf parsley (coarsely chopped)
1 teaspoon of nigella seeds
12 sheets of filo dough
    (each 6 x 8 inches/15 x 20 cm)
Extra-virgin olive oil for brushing

After a day of fasting during Ramadan, we eat soup with sambusak—crispy pastry rolls filled with either cheese or meat (see page 74). As soon as you dip a roll into the soup, the cravings of the day melt away and are quickly forgotten.

Traditional sambusak dough is made by hand, filled with akawi cheese (a mild Middle Eastern white cheese) and deep fried. My version is quicker, lighter, and made with ingredients that are more readily available outside of the Middle East. Even with these substitutions, the result is quite similar to the original.

Sambusak
— Filo Rolls with Meat Filling

In a pan, heat the oil over medium heat. Fry the onion in the hot oil for about 3 minutes, or until soft. Add the ground meat to the onion, breaking it into small pieces with a wooden spoon. Brown for 5 minutes, or until it is completely cooked and the moisture has evaporated.

Add the cilantro, pine nuts, pomegranate molasses, and allspice. Add salt and pepper to taste, and fry for another 2 minutes. Set aside to cool.

Form the rolls: Place a sheet of filo dough flat in front of you. Spoon a tablespoon of the filling onto the sheet, about 2 inches (5 cm) from the edge closest to you. Fold the edge over the filling and press the filo dough down with a moistened finger so that it sticks. Then fold the side edges towards the inside. Roll up the filled filo dough like a cigar to form the pastry roll. Seal the seams with a little bit of water. The roll should be about 3 inches (8 cm) long. Repeat using the rest of the filling and filo dough.

Preheat the oven to 400°F (200°C). Grease a baking sheet with olive oil.

Arrange the rolls on the prepared sheet, making sure they are not touching. Brush the filo rolls with olive oil. Bake for 15 minutes, turning them occasionally so that they crisp evenly. They should be golden brown on all sides.

MAKES 12

1 tablespoon of extra-virgin olive oil,
  plus extra for brushing
1 onion (chopped)
9 oz (250 g) of ground beef
1 bunch of cilantro (finely chopped)
2 tablespoons of pine nuts (toasted)
2 tablespoons of pomegranate molasses
1 teaspoon of ground allspice
Salt and pepper
12 sheets of filo dough
  (each 6 x 8 inches/15 x 20 cm)

For most Syrians, myself included, these pastries are a quintessential Ramadan treat, often eaten with soup. My sisters and I always fought over who would get the last roll! A Ramadan menu always has something a bit more special about it, and is just a touch more varied than the usual dinner spread (see page 207). My mother only made these rolls for Ramadan, which was not entirely a bad thing because they are very hard to resist!

Sfeeha
— Mini-Flatbreads with Ground Beef

FIRST, MAKE THE MEAT FILLING
Process the onion, garlic, tomatoes, and parsley in a
food processor until it is a smooth purée.

In a bowl, mix the ground meat, tomato paste,
paprika, crushed red pepper flakes, pomegranate
molasses, oil, salt, and pepper. Add the purée from
the food processor. Knead everything by hand until
the ingredients are evenly incorporated.

DOUGH—FIRST STEP
In a large bowl, mix the yeast with the sugar. Whisk
in the warm water until the yeast and sugar have
dissolved. Gradually add the flour and mix until
completely incorporated, with no visible lumps in the
dough. Cover the bowl with a tea towel and set aside
to rise for 15 minutes.

DOUGH—SECOND STEP
Add the yogurt, oil, flour, and salt to the dough.
Knead it by hand for 7–10 minutes, until smooth,
soft, and elastic. Add some extra flour to the dough
if it sticks to your hands.

Lightly flour your work surface. Divide the dough
into 16 pieces, each about the size of an egg. Form
into balls, and then roll them into circles measuring
4–4½ inches (10–12 cm) in diameter. Spread a thin
layer of the meat filling over each circle of dough.

Line a baking sheet with parchment paper, then heat
a nonstick frying pan over medium heat. Arrange the
sfeehas in the pan, filling side up, without
overcrowding the pan (you will need to work in
batches). Fry for 2 minutes.

INGREDIENTS

MAKES 16

FOR THE MEAT FILLING
2 onions (quartered)
3 garlic cloves (peeled)
2 tomatoes (halved)
1 bunch of flat-leaf parsley, plus extra to serve
10½ oz (300 g) of ground beef
1 tablespoon of tomato paste
1 tablespoon of paprika
1 tablespoon of crushed red pepper flakes
1 tablespoon of pomegranate molasses
2 tablespoons of extra-virgin olive oil
Salt and pepper

DOUGH—FIRST STEP
1 envelope (7 g) of instant yeast
2 teaspoons of sugar
Generous ¾ cup (200 ml) of warm water
1 cup (125 g) of all-purpose flour

DOUGH—SECOND STEP
¼ cup (75 g) of Greek yogurt
2 tablespoons of vegetable oil
2¼ cups (275 g) of all-purpose flour, plus extra for dusting
1 teaspoon of salt
—
Food processor

Transfer the fried sfeehas to the prepared baking
sheet and broil for 3 minutes. Repeat with the
remaining sfeehas. Finishing them under the broiler
will ensure that your sfeehas are tender in texture.

They are delicious with lemon slices and parsley.

Sfeeha

This flatbread is similar to Turkish pizza, though the toppings are different. In Syria, we have two different toppings: a meat one and a "vegetable" one, though confusingly, this also contains meat. What's the difference, you might ask? The meat topping has only meat. The vegetable topping contains vegetables mixed into the meat.

Where there are sfeehas, there is a party. Traditionally, if a celebration was coming up, the meat would be ordered from the butcher, seasoned with the family recipe, then brought to the local community oven, called the ferran. This is where the dough bases for the flatbreads were prepared—just the right number for the amount of spiced meat (more meat, more circles!). The sfeehas would be baked there. Coming home with one or two hundred sfeehas was more the rule than the exception! Imagine that many, set on the table in towering, appetizing stacks!

Mortadella from Aleppo
— Beef Sausage with Garlic and Pistachios

PREPARATION

In a large bowl, knead together the beef, breadcrumbs, garlic, egg, allspice, and salt, until smooth. This is traditionally done by hand, but it can also be done in a free-standing mixer using the dough hook. This makes the consistency even smoother.

Divide the meat mixture into four equal balls and, using the palm of your hand, flatten each ball to a round that is about ¾ inch (2 cm) thick.

Divide the pistachios into four equal portions—one portion per meat round. Place the pistachios into the middle of round. Wet your hands slightly and then roll each round into an oval sausage shape. Place the sausages on a baking sheet and refrigerate for least 30 minutes so they become a bit firmer.

In the meantime, combine the vinegar and water to fill a large pot. Bring to a boil. Place the mortadella in the boiling liquid and boil the sausages for 20–25 minutes, until cooked through.

Using a slotted spoon, transfer the sausages to a plate and refrigerate until completely cool. Once cool, slice them into ½ inch (1 cm) thick slices.

Serve with bread and a squeeze of lemon juice.

INGREDIENTS

MAKES 4

1 lb 2 oz (500 g) of lean ground beef
¼ cup (30 g) of fine breadcrumbs
6 garlic cloves (4 pressed,
   and 2 thinly sliced)
1 egg
1½ teaspoons of ground allspice
1 teaspoon of salt
3 tablespoons of chopped pistachios

TO BLANCH THE SAUSAGE
4 parts water and 1 part apple cider vinegar

TO SERVE
Flatbread
Lemon wedges

Cold cuts are all called "mortadella" in Syria. You might say that this refers to the meat Syrians eat in sandwiches. As kids we ate canned mortadella on bread, preferably with ketchup. But once my mother realized what we were eating, she substituted the canned sausage with this homemade version. Over the years, my tastes have evolved somewhat and I think this homemade sausage is much tastier than the canned favorite of my childhood. A squeeze of lemon over the mortadella is akin to magic.

Laban bi khyar
— Yogurt with Cucumber and Garlic

PREPARATION

Combine all the ingredients in a bowl. Gently mix, adding salt to taste. Serve cold, drizzled with extra-virgin olive oil and sprinkled with mint leaves. Enjoy as a dipping sauce or as a side to pilaf dishes.

INGREDIENTS

SERVES 4

1⅔ cups (400 g) of Greek yogurt
½ Persian or Lebanese cucumber (very thinly sliced)
2 garlic cloves (pressed)
Juice of 1 organic lemon
1 tablespoon of dried mint or
   1 bunch of fresh mint (finely chopped)
Salt

TO SERVE
Extra-virgin olive oil
Mint leaves

All Middle Eastern, Balkan, and South Asian countries have a signature version of this dip. The Greeks eat tzatziki, Indians eat raita. The Syrian version uses Syrian yogurt, distinctive because it is a bit thicker than most yogurts and has a citrusy freshness. In this recipe, I use Greek yogurt because it is readily available. This creamy dip goes perfectly with pilaf dishes such as mujaddara (see page 128) and makloube (see page 151).

Muhammara
— Spicy Red Pepper–Walnut Dip

In a food processor, blend all the ingredients together for about 2 minutes. The mixture should be thick, with some texture from the walnuts. Taste and add salt.

This dip will keep well in the refrigerator, but should be served at room temperature. Drizzle with extra-virgin olive oil and pomegranate molasses and garnish with chopped parsley and walnuts before serving.

INGREDIENTS

SERVES 4

5½ oz (150 g) roasted red peppers from a jar
1 teaspoon of red pepper paste
1 hot red chili pepper
⅔ cup (75 g) of walnut pieces
½ cup (50 g) of plain breadcrumbs
2 tablespoons of extra-virgin olive oil
1 tablespoon of pomegranate molasses
Juice of ½ organic lemon
Salt

TO SERVE
Extra-virgin olive oil
Pomegranate molasses
Small handful of flat-leaf parsley (coarsely chopped)
Small handful of walnuts (coarsely chopped)
—
Food processor

My love for muhammara is all-encompassing. I'm especially fond of mixing muhammara and hummus together (see pages 60 and 61). Give it a try! The secret to the best muhammara is in the red pepper paste, which is made with slow-roasted and dried red peppers, concentrating their flavor. The red pepper paste can be omitted if necessary, but it is worth the effort to find it! Try Middle Eastern and Turkish grocery stores (it is usually sold in tubes).

STREET FOOD

We roamed the city streets, from the old souks to the modern markets, from one neighborhood to another, going from cafés to baklava shops.

Boys' night out

—

Summer vacations for me, as a twelve-year-old boy, and, later, as an adolescent, were lived as one moment of freedom followed by another, the likes of which didn't happen at any other time of the year. As soon as I got the chance, I would meet up with a bunch of my many cousins and friends. Some twenty-five of them lived close by, so there were always a few who were keen to go out. We mostly took advantage of the times our parents had a wedding to go to or had some other festivities planned. (Invitations would come printed with the saying "a child's home is heaven," a diplomatic and typically Syrian way to say that children were not invited.) And that's how boys' night out was born.

These outings revolved around one thing, and one thing only: street food. I got the chance to try whatever I wanted. In those days, Homs was a big city of 650,000 people. After sunset, once it had cooled down a bit, the city came to life. And so it was in this hustle and bustle, while sitting on front stoops or in plastic chairs, or while walking from take-out joint to corner kiosk, that I got to know the many faces of Syrian street food. My favorites were toshka, shawarma, and ma'aleh (sandwiches of meat and cheese, grilled meat, and deep-fried vegetables). We roamed the city streets, from the old souks to the modern markets, from one neighborhood to another. Going from cafés to baklava shops, we would eat until we couldn't eat any more. And then we would play cards or a pick-up game of soccer or tennis.

At first, my parents gave me spending money for these adventures. Once I was a bit older, though, my cousins and I did try to find jobs, even though that wasn't a typical thing for Syrian teenagers to do. I remember one summer when a cousin of mine and I started our own "shop." We would buy grocery items from another store and then resell them. Chocolate, chips . . . that sort of thing. We posted losses because we tended to eat the inventory. Later on we got jobs packaging medicine at a pharmacy, a side job that my uncle arranged for us. We weren't really that motivated, however, so the jobs didn't last long. But, for the time it did last, we invested the wages we earned directly back into Homs' street-food scene.

Those midsummer evenings, full of spontaneous and uncomplicated adventures in the city that embraced us, gave me a great sense of freedom and friendship. I learned to love Syrian food in all its forms. My memories of that time are fond ones.

Batinjan bi hamud
— Sour Roasted Eggplant

PREPARATION

Preheat the oven to 480°F (250°C).

Arrange the eggplant slices on a baking sheet and brush or rub them with 2 tablespoons of the extra-virgin olive oil. Salt the eggplant well and roast in the oven for 20–25 minutes, or until golden brown and somewhat charred at the edges.

In a small bowl, mix the tomato, garlic, parsley, lemon juice, and the remaining 1 tablespoon of olive oil. Add salt to taste.

Place two pieces of the roasted eggplant on each plate and add some of the tomato salad. Drizzle with pomegranate molasses and sprinkle with fresh pomegranate seeds.

INGREDIENTS

SERVES 4

2 eggplants (cut lengthwise into four wedges)
3 tablespoons of extra-virgin olive oil
Salt
2 tomatoes (diced)
2 garlic cloves (pressed)
1 bunch of flat-leaf parsley (finely chopped)
Juice of 1 organic lemon
2 tablespoons of pomegranate molasses
1 handful of pomegranate seeds

This is a modified version of a street-food sandwich. I've turned it into a side dish here. And, instead of deep-frying the eggplant wedges, they are roasted in the oven. The lemon, pomegranate molasses, and pomegranate seeds give the dish an amazing sweet-sour flavor. It goes well with everything!

Falafel

Syrians never make falafel at home—at least my mother never did. There are numerous falafel joints, some better than others, all cheap. So why would you make it? Nowadays I do make my own falafel, to capture the flavor of Syria.

I make up a batch, with an assortment of fresh herbs mixed in, when I am having friends over. Everyone picks from the heaped plate of falafel, and smaller plates of pickles, vegetables, sauce, and flatbread, and puts together their own sandwiches.

Falafel

PREPARATION

Soak the chickpeas in cold water overnight, or for at least 12 hours. The chickpeas should swell to twice their size and should feel soft. Drain and rinse.

In a food processor, combine the drained chickpeas, parsley, cilantro, onion, garlic, chili pepper, cumin, olive oil, salt, and pepper and process for about 2 minutes. The mixture should be well blended, but not too smooth.

Form the mixture into small balls measuring about 1¼ inches (3 cm) in diameter. Sprinkle them lightly with sesame seeds, and using your fingertips, gently press the seeds into the falafel. Refrigerate the falafel for 30 minutes.

In a large pot, pour in the oil to a depth of about 2 inches (5 cm) and heat the oil to 350°F (180°C). If you don't have a kitchen thermometer, test-fry a falafel ball to see if the oil is hot enough (it should bubble vigorously around the falafel). Line a large plate or baking sheet with paper towels and set aside.

Deep-fry a few falafel at a time to keep from overcrowding the pot. Fry for 5–6 minutes, or until brown and cooked through. Using a slotted spoon, transfer the cooked falafel to the lined plate or pan to drain excess oil. Falafel are good with tarator (page 21) or in a pita sandwich with a lot of lettuce.

INGREDIENTS

MAKES 30–35

1 cup (200 g) of dried chickpeas
1 bunch of flat-leaf parsley, stems included
1 bunch of cilantro, stems included
1 onion (peeled, cut into quarters)
3 garlic cloves (peeled)
1 green chili pepper
½ teaspoon of ground cumin
2 tablespoons of extra-virgin olive oil
½ teaspoon of salt, or to taste
½ teaspoon of ground black pepper
3 tablespoons of sesame seeds
Vegetable oil for frying
—
Food processor

Falafel is usually deep-fried, which has given them a reputation as a greasy, unhealthy (and delicious) snack. It's common to hear a Syrian ask someone who has a case of the hiccups: "Did you eat falafel yesterday?"

Beef shawarma

In a large bowl, knead the sliced beef with the kiwi and half of the lemon juice for 2 minutes to tenderize the meat.

Add the rest of the ingredients and continue mixing until the meat is evenly coated with the marinade. Cover and refrigerate for at least 3 hours, preferably overnight, to give time for the flavors to develop.

Preheat the oven to 400°F (200°C).

Spread the beef and its marinade evenly on a baking sheet. Roast the shawarma for 15–20 minutes—the meat should have the beginnings of a crispy coating, but should still be juicy.

Fill a flatbread with some of the meat, fresh tomato, and biwaz salad. Finish with a generous helping of tarator on top. Roll up and enjoy!

INGREDIENTS

SERVES 4

1 lb 5 oz (600 g) of beef steak (thinly sliced)

1 ripe kiwi (peeled and coarsely chopped)

Juice of 1 organic lemon

5–7 garlic cloves (pressed)

2 tablespoons of white wine vinegar

1 bunch of fresh thyme

4 teaspoons of 7 spices blend (see page 15)

½ teaspoon of Aleppo pepper or cayenne pepper

2 tablespoons of extra-virgin olive oil

1 teaspoon salt, or to taste

TO SERVE
Flatbread
Tomato slices
Biwaz (page 135)
Tarator (page 21)

Shawarma

In Syria, shawarma is sold from small kiosks, not any
larger than the cooking area itself. The kiosks open
as evening starts. Shawarma is the only thing on the
menu and every shawarma stand uses its own recipe
that the "teacher" (that is what the malem, or head
chef, is called) guards with their life. Not even their
own staff know what goes into it. You might stand
in line for 45 minutes to get a good shawarma.
And then, finally, shawarma in hand, you find a front
stoop or some stairs close by to sit on and eat it
on the spot. The pre-packaged shawarma that you can
sometimes buy in supermarkets doesn't even come
close to Syrian shawarma. Not only is the ready-
made stuff dry, some of it is made from pork.
Authentic shawarma is made from chicken or beef.
The layers of fat in between the meat fibers are what
keep the meat juicy as it is hung on the vertical spit.
I serve my shawarma rolled up in a flatbread with
biwaz (page 135) and tarator (page 21).

Zahra
— Spicy Roasted Cauliflower

PREPARATION

Preheat the oven to 425°F (220°C).

On a large baking sheet, toss the cauliflower florets and any leaves with the olive oil, cumin, paprika, and some salt. Bake for approximately 25–30 minutes, or until golden brown and just starting to char at the tips.

Take the cauliflower out of the oven, toss with the garlic, and bake for another 5 minutes.

Serve zahra, street food-style, in a pita or flatbread sandwich, stuffed with fresh herbs and tarator, or as a snack or side dish, with tarator for dipping.

INGREDIENTS

SERVES 6

1 cauliflower (cut into florets, leaves reserved)
3 tablespoons of extra-virgin olive oil
2 teaspoons of ground cumin
2 teaspoons of ground paprika
Salt
3 garlic cloves (pressed)

TO SERVE
Pita or Middle Eastern flatbread
Fresh herbs of your choice
Tarator (page 21)

Ma'aleh is usually deep-fried cauliflower, served in a sandwich with raw vegetables and tarator (page 21). Most Syrians eat cauliflower this way, but any vegetable can be made into ma'aleh—just deep-fry it and make a sandwich as described above. But in my opinion, my mother's oven-roasted cauliflower is even better; it's a perfect side dish or sandwich filling.

STREET FOOD

Toshka
— Toasted Sandwiches with Spicy Meat and Cheese

PREPARATION

Combine the ground lamb or beef, garlic, parsley, cayenne pepper, crushed red pepper flakes, cumin, salt, and pepper. Knead all ingredients together until well incorporated.

Slice open the pita bread. On the bottom half, place a thin layer of ground beef and then layer with two of the cheese slices. Repeat with the remaining pitas. Close the sandwiches and lightly press the halves together.

Heat a frying pan over medium heat and cook the toshkas for 3–5 minutes on each side. Cut them into triangles and serve with toum and pickles.

INGREDIENTS

MAKES 4

1 lb 2 oz (500 g) of ground lamb or beef
5 garlic cloves (pressed)
1 bunch of flat-leaf parsley (finely chopped)
4 teaspoons of cayenne pepper
1 teaspoon of crushed red pepper flakes
1 teaspoon of ground cumin
½ teaspoon of salt, or to taste
Pinch of ground black pepper
4 pita breads or Middle Eastern flatbreads
8 thin slices (5½ oz/150 g in total)
   of Kashkaval or Gouda cheese

TO SERVE (OPTIONAL)
Toum (Middle Eastern garlic aioli)
Pickles

As children, a cousin of mine and I especially loved toshkas. Our family's favorite toshka stand was in a neighborhood with a lot of feral cats roaming around. My cousin and I thought that this specific stand's meat was so good, and it tasted so different from the meat we had tasted elsewhere, that we convinced ourselves that it must be cat meat. Of course this wasn't the case at all—it was simply well-seasoned beef or lamb, the secret of any tasty toshka. The other key to a good toshka is cheese, in all its gooey goodness.

Lob el kossa
— Pan-Fried Zucchini with Garlic and Mint

Heat the oil in a nonstick pan over high heat and sauté the zucchini with the garlic for 5–7 minutes, or until seared.

Add the mint, ground paprika, lemon juice, and a pinch of salt and pepper. Continue to cook, stirring, for another minute.

Serve the zucchini as a warm side dish, drizzled with extra-virgin olive oil and garnished with fresh mint.

SERVES 2

2 tablespoons of extra-virgin olive oil
1 large zucchini (halved lengthwise)
3 garlic cloves (thinly sliced)
2 teaspoons of dried mint
1 teaspoon of paprika
Juice of 1 organic lemon
Salt and pepper

TO SERVE
Extra-virgin olive oil
Fresh mint leaves

In the Arab world, and most certainly in Syria, we love stuffed vegetables, especially zucchini. This simple side dish was inspired by a dish usually made to use up the leftover scooped out zucchini flesh, but I use the whole zucchini here. Serve it in pita to make ma'aleh (see also zahra, page 98), one of my favorite street foods.

GRAINS, VEGETABLES,
AND MORE

I clearly remember my grandfather sitting at his kitchen table, the radio tuned to the broadcast of the Monte Carlo. In the evenings, he always listened to the news first, and then to the music of Umm Kulthum.

Warm dishes for a winter spread
—

Winter in Amsterdam, the city I now call home, is a time to savor the warmth of good company gathered around the dining table. I like to invite people over, preferably a whole kitchen full. The best part is seating as many as can fit along both sides of my 8-foot (2.5-meter) dining room table! My friends hail from all corners of the globe—Asia, North and South America, Europe, and the Middle East—and I feed them Syrian-style, with a rich assortment of dishes meant to be shared. I feed them as my mother and my grandmother taught me.

I clearly remember my grandfather sitting at his kitchen table, the radio tuned to the broadcast of the Monte Carlo. In the evenings, he always listened to the news first, and then to the music of Umm Kulthum, the legendary Egyptian singer. Her music was on the radio every night, without fail.

The old Arabic music she was famous for is soft and melodious, and so calming and hypnotic. Listening to the same music while I cook a winter meal creates the perfect cozy ambience. There is nothing like this music to put me in the right winter mood.

Humming to the music, I blend hummus, and I make a variety of other dips. A pot of pea soup simmers. Yes, this consummate Dutch dish, made from ingredients that couldn't be easier to find, but prepared with Middle Eastern spices. I use these winter get-togethers as times to experiment, though everything I make is grounded in memory. Old and new meet, the international is made local. I don't confine myself to any particular group; I belong everywhere and nowhere at the same time. Even so, as I sit at the winter table in the company of delightful people and delicious food, I feel completely at home.

Fattoush
— Famous Toasted Bread Salad

PREPARATION

In a small bowl, use a fork to whisk together all the dressing ingredients except for the sumac.

In a large bowl, and using clean hands, toss all the salad ingredients except the flatbread pieces. Add the dressing, 1 teaspoon of the sumac, and toss. Let the salad rest to meld the flavors.

Before serving, arrange the toasted flatbread croutons over the salad and sprinkle the other teaspoon of sumac over the entire dish.

———

*In Syria, purslane is often used in fattoush. Try it if you can find it in your local farmers' market.

INGREDIENTS

SERVES 4

1 head of romaine lettuce*
  (washed and cut up into large pieces)
½ a small cucumber (chopped)
3 medium tomatoes (chopped)
3 radishes (thinly sliced)
1 red onion (halved and sliced into thin rings)
1 bunch of flat-leaf parsley (coarsely chopped)
1 bunch of mint (coarsely chopped)
1 flatbread (toasted and broken into pieces)

FOR THE DRESSING
1 garlic clove (pressed)
Juice of 1 organic lemon
2 tablespoons of white wine vinegar
1 tablespoon of pomegranate molasses
Scant ½ cup (100 ml) of good quality
  extra-virgin olive oil
Pinch of salt
2 teaspoons of sumac

This is a well-known dish in Syrian cuisine. There is no single "authentic" way to prepare it, nor does the dish have a fixed ingredient list. It's improvisational and as simple as chopping up some salad greens and serving them with a dressing. That's it. It's the toasted flatbread on top that makes it fattoush. Despite its variability, this dish tastes of Syria like none other. It tastes like the country, like the earth, like the local, and the regional. It tastes like a hundred stories. A beautiful dish.

Fasolia bi zeit
— Green Beans in Tomato and Olive Oil Sauce

PREPARATION

Heat the oil in a pan with deep sides on medium heat. Fry the onion, minced and sliced garlic, and chili pepper for 4–5 minutes until soft but not browned.

Add the tomatoes, and season with salt and pepper to taste. Simmer for another 5 minutes.

Stir the green beans into the sauce. Turn the heat to low, cover, and simmer until the beans are cooked, about 15 minutes. The beans will release moisture.

Drizzle liberally with extra-virgin olive oil. Serve warm or at room temperature as a side dish or light main dish, accompanied by warm flatbread.

INGREDIENTS

SERVES 4

Scant ½ cup (100 ml) of extra-virgin olive oil
2 onions (coarsely chopped)
8 garlic cloves (3 minced, and 5 thinly sliced)
1 red or yellow chili pepper (chopped or sliced open)
3 tomatoes (diced)
Salt and pepper
1 lb (500 g) of string beans or flat green beans
    (stems trimmed, halved lengthwise)

TO SERVE
Good quality extra-virgin olive oil
Middle Eastern flatbread (optional)

In Arabic, this dish is literally called "green beans with olive oil." It is a vegetarian appetizer that can be eaten at room temperature, and is usually served with a basket of flatbread. Quite a bit of garlic is added. I make a point of using some whole garlic cloves, a rebellion of sorts, but you can follow the recipe and use sliced and minced garlic as called for.

Shorbat adas
— Traditional Red Lentil Soup

Heat the oil in a large pot over medium heat. Fry the onion for about 5 minutes until soft and light golden brown. Push the onion to the side of the pan and add the turmeric, cumin, and cayenne pepper. Fry the spices for 1 minute—the frying releases the aromas of the spices and imparts an extra dimension to the flavors of this dish.

Add the lentils to the pot and stir well. Add the stock and bring to a boil. Turn the heat to low, cover, and simmer the lentils for 20 minutes, stirring occasionally to keep them from burning or sticking to the bottom of the pot. The lentils should be completely cooked.

Using a handheld immersion blender, purée the soup until smooth. Add the lemon juice, and salt and pepper to taste. If the soup is too thick, add some extra stock or water. Cook the soup for another 5 minutes on low heat to heat through.

Ladle the soup into deep serving bowls, top with sumac, parsley, and nigella seeds, and serve with lemon wedges.

SERVES 6

4 tablespoons of extra-virgin olive oil
4 onions (chopped)
½ teaspoon of ground turmeric
½ teaspoon of ground cumin
1 tablespoon of cayenne pepper
2⅓ cups (450 g) of red lentils (rinsed)
7½ cups (1.75 liters) of chicken
  or vegetable stock
Juice of 1 organic lemon
Salt and pepper

TO SERVE
1 tablespoon of sumac
1 small handful of flat-leaf parsley
  (coarsely chopped)
1 tablespoon of nigella seeds
1 organic lemon (cut into wedges)
—
Handheld immersion blender

There are countless ways to make lentil soup. In Syria, we used to eat either brown or red lentil soup during Ramadan. Now that I live in Amsterdam, I eat this dish more often—it helps me get through the cold Dutch winters. My version is spicier than the soups you can find in restaurants here. Don't forget the lemon juice because the citrusy kick brings it to another level.

Itsch salad
— Aunt Jinan's Bulgur Salad

PREPARATION

Heat the olive oil in a large pot and fry the onion for 5 minutes, or until soft.

Add the tomato paste and fry for 2 more minutes.

Add the bulgur and boiling water to the onion mixture. Turn the heat to low, cover, and simmer for 5 minutes, until all the water has been absorbed. Remove from the heat and leave to cool.

Once cool, stir in the olive oil, pomegranate molasses, lemon juice, and dried mint, and add salt and pepper to taste. Mix in the scallions, tomatoes, and parsley.

Spoon the salad into a large bowl. Smooth the top using the rounded part of the spoon. Drizzle it with some extra-virgin olive oil and pomegranate molasses, letting both pool in some of the grooves formed by the spoon. Enjoy!

INGREDIENTS

SERVES 4

2 tablespoons of extra-virgin olive oil
1 large onion (chopped)
2 tablespoons of tomato paste
1½ cups (225 g) of fine bulgur (rinsed)
1 cup (250 ml) of boiling water
Generous ¾ cup (200 ml) of extra-virgin olive oil,
    plus extra to serve
4 tablespoons of pomegranate molasses,
    plus extra to serve
Juice of 1 organic lemon
1 tablespoon of crumbled dried mint
Salt and pepper
2 scallions (chopped)
2 tomatoes (diced)
1 large bunch of flat-leaf parsley
    (coarsely chopped)

This tabouleh variation uses almost all the same ingredients as a regular tabouleh, but where there is usually more parsley than bulgur, itsch switches those proportions and uses more bulgur than parsley. It comes from the city of Aleppo, which is evident from the recipe's name. Itsch, pronounced "itsjie," immediately conjures Aleppo to the mind of an Arabic speaker because the sound "itsj" is characteristic of their local dialect. It may be just a coincidence, but it makes sense to me—itsch salad sounds like it's from Aleppo!

Mkhallal
— Spicy Pickles

PREPARATION

Choose which pickle you are making. Mix together
the ingredients for the vinegar brine. If your jar is
larger or if you just want to make more jars of
pickles, increase amounts listed for the brine
ingredients, keeping the same proportions. An
opened jar of pickles will keep refrigerated for
6 months.

PICKLED CUCUMBERS
Fill the jar with cucumbers, leaving room at the top.
Tuck the garlic and chili pepper halves in between
and around the cucumbers. Pour in as much of the
vinegar brine as is necessary to completely cover
the cucumbers. Put the lid on the jar and let the
cucumbers pickle at room temperature for at least
7 days.

PICKLED TURNIPS
You can make the popular Syrian pink turnip pickles
the same way as described above—just substitute
turnips for cucumbers and add a couple of beet
segments to the jar.

PICKLED STUFFED RED PEPPERS
Mix together the cabbage, carrot, and finely chopped
pepper, then fill the 2 whole red peppers with
this mixture.

Put the peppers tight up against each other in the jar
and tuck the garlic and chili pepper halves in between
and around them. Pour in as much of the vinegar
brine as is necessary to completely cover the peppers.
Put the lid on the jar and let the peppers pickle
at room temperature for at least 7 days.

INGREDIENTS

FOR ONE 1-QUART (1-LITER) JAR OF
ONE OF THE FOLLOWING PICKLES

VINEGAR BRINE
1 cup (250 ml) of water
⅓ cup (75 ml) of white vinegar
1 tablespoon of salt
½ teaspoon of sugar

PICKLED CUCUMBERS
8 Persian or baby cucumbers
1 garlic clove (halved)
1 hot chili pepper (halved)

PICKLED TURNIPS
2 turnips (peeled and cut into segments)
1 small boiled beet (cut into segments)
1 garlic clove (halved)
1 hot chili pepper (halved)

PICKLED STUFFED RED PEPPERS
¼ cabbage (diced)
1 carrot (thinly sliced)
3 red peppers (1 finely chopped,
   2 left whole, with stems and seeds removed)
1 garlic clove (halved)
1 hot chili pepper (halved)

We always had pickles in our pantry, either the ones my grandmother made from the vegetables she grew, or the ones that were sold just about anywhere you looked. I had never stopped to reflect on pickles, or what they might mean to me, until I moved away from Syria. I just couldn't get used to western-style pickles; they were way too sweet. Since moving to the Netherlands, I've been making them in my grandmother's style. One particular favorite is the whole red pepper pickle in vinegar. To serve, cut it into segments.

Sheikh mushatah
— Grilled Eggplants with Yogurt Sauce

PREPARATION

Preheat the broiler.

Rub the eggplant halves with olive oil and
then liberally sprinkle with salt and pepper. Broil for
20–30 minutes until they are cooked and the edges
are somewhat charred. You can also do this on
the grill.

For the sauce, mix the yogurt, tahini, lemon
juice, and garlic in a bowl. Thin the mixture with
2–4 tablespoons of water. Add salt to taste.

Make the salad by tossing the tomato and parsley
with extra-virgin olive oil and lemon zest.

Arrange the grilled eggplant halves on a plate
or in a large dish, top them first with the yogurt sauce
and then the green tarator (or zhoug if you love spicy
food). Sprinkle with the tomato-parsley salad and
toasted pine nuts.

INGREDIENTS

SERVES 4

2 eggplants (halved lengthwise)
2 tablespoons of extra-virgin olive oil
Salt and pepper

FOR THE YOGURT SAUCE
⅔ cup (150 g) of Greek yogurt
3 tablespoons of tahini
Juice of 1 organic lemon
2 garlic cloves (pressed)
Salt

TO SERVE
1 tomato (diced)
1 handful of flat-leaf parsley (chopped)
1 tablespoon of extra-virgin olive oil
Zest of 1 organic lemon
4 tablespoons of green tarator
  or zhoug (pages 20–21)
2 tablespoons of pine nuts (toasted)

*In Arabic, this recipe is literally called "the sheikh who
lays on his back." The sheikh is the eggplant, which is
so important in Syrian cuisine. Combined with garlic
yogurt (which is delicious on practically everything),
you have one of the best dishes ever! The ingredients are
similar to those in moutabal (page 48), but because the
eggplants are broiled rather than charred over an open
flame, the flavors are completely different.*

Horak osbao
— Lentil and Pasta Stew with Tamarind and Pomegranate

PREPARATION

Heat a scant ½ cup (100 ml) of the olive oil in a large nonstick pot over medium heat.

Cook the onion rings, stirring frequently, for about 15 minutes, until dark brown and caramelized. Take care to not have the heat set too high because onions burn easily.

Line a plate with paper towels. Remove half of the caramelized onions from the pot and place them on the paper towels to drain the excess oil.

Add the lentils and chicken stock to the onions left in the pot. Bring to a boil, reduce the heat, and boil gently for 20 minutes, or until tender.

Add the fettuccine, pomegranate molasses, tamarind paste, and lemon juice. Cook for another 10 minutes, adding more water if needed. It should be thick and saucy, but not too watery. Turn the heat off when the pasta is tender. Cover and let rest for 10 minutes, or until the remaining moisture is absorbed.

Meanwhile, heat the remaining 3½ tablespoons (50 ml) of oil in a nonstick pan on medium heat. Fry the garlic until golden. Stir in the chopped cilantro (reserving some for the garnish) and fry for another 1 minute.

Stir the fried garlic and cilantro into the horak osbao. Add salt and pepper to taste, and sprinkle with the reserved fried onions and chopped cilantro. Make it even tastier by topping it with some pomegranate seeds and serving it with lemon wedges.

INGREDIENTS

SERVES 4–6

⅔ cup (150 ml) of extra-virgin olive oil
4 red onions (sliced into thin rings)
1¼ cups (250 g) of green lentils (rinsed)
3 cups (750 ml) of chicken stock
5½ oz (150 g) of fettuccine (broken into pieces)
3 tablespoons of pomegranate molasses
2 tablespoons of tamarind paste
Juice of 1 organic lemon
7 garlic cloves (pressed)
1 large bunch of cilantro
   (coarsely chopped)
Salt and pepper

TO SERVE
Pomegranate seeds
1 organic lemon (cut into wedges)

The Arabic name for this dish, hora'a bi osba'o, literally means "burned fingers." As the story goes, the first person to have discovered how delicious this dish is could not wait for it to cool down before tasting it. Try it at your own risk!

Syrian cuisine is still quite regional. Since this dish is from Damascus, and my family is from Homs, it is not part of my family's repertoire of recipes. In fact, I didn't taste it for the first time until I was at university! It's a bit strange to think I hadn't encountered it before then, but ever since that first taste, it's been one of my favorites. I make it often at home.

Mom's famous beet salad

PREPARATION

Combine all ingredients for the dressing and add salt and pepper to taste.

In a large bowl or serving dish, combine the beets, onions, and spinach. Using your hands, toss well with the dressing. Sprinkle with the walnuts and serve immediately.

INGREDIENTS

SERVES 4

1 lb 2 oz (500 g) of cooked beets (thinly sliced)
2 red onions (sliced in thin rings)
7 oz (200 g) of baby spinach
½ cup (50 g) of walnut pieces

FOR THE DRESSING
2 garlic cloves (pressed)
2 tablespoons of apple cider vinegar
Zest or juice of 1 organic lemon
Generous ¾ cup (200 ml) of extra-virgin olive oil
Salt and pepper

This is my mother's favorite. She is crazy about beets, even if the rest of her family (talking about you, Dad) doesn't share her enthusiasm. My mother, like other mothers, tends to make what the other family members enjoy eating, and in so doing, forgets to make her own favorites. Nevertheless, my mother would treat herself to this salad once in a while, and, not forgetting my father, would cobble together something else for him to eat.

Mujaddara
— Lentil Pilaf with Caramelized Onions

PREPARATION

Heat the oil in a large nonstick pot over medium heat.
Fry the onion rings for about 15 minutes, stirring
regularly, until they caramelize and turn dark brown.
Do not have the heat set too high because onions
burn easily.

Line a plate with paper towels. Remove half of the
caramelized onions from the pot and place them
on the paper towels to drain the excess oil.

Push the remaining onions to one side of the pot, add
the allspice and cumin, and toast the spices for about
1 minute. Add the lentils, along with enough water to
cover them by ½ inch (1 cm). Bring to a boil, then
lower the heat and simmer for about 15 minutes,
or until semi-cooked.

Mix in the uncooked rice and add more water until
the rice and lentil mixture is covered by ½ inch
(1 cm). Add the salt and pepper. Bring to a boil and
then turn heat to low. Simmer the mujaddara for
about 12 minutes, or until all the water has been
absorbed and the rice is cooked.

Take the pan off the heat, cover the pot, and let the
mujaddara rest for 5 minutes. Serve warm, topped
with the reserved fried onions.

INGREDIENTS

SERVES 6

4 tablespoons of extra-virgin olive oil
5 large white onions (sliced in thin rings)
½ tablespoon of ground allspice
½ tablespoon of ground cumin
Heaped 1 cup (225 g) of dried brown lentils (rinsed)
1¼ cups (225 g) of long-grain white rice
(rinsed and soaked in water for
approximately 20 minutes)
1 teaspoon salt, or to taste
1 teaspoon ground black pepper, or to taste

*Many would call this dish "poor man's food," but I call
it "simply the best." There's not much more to it than
rice, lentils, and onions. Even so, it all comes together
to make something amazing, nutritious, and satisfying.
Sometimes this pilaf is made with bulgur instead of
rice, though I prefer it with rice. It is delicious with the
yogurt-cucumber dip, laban bi khyar (page 80).*

Yalanji

Who invented yalanji? Lots of places claim that honor, and it is eaten with abandon in many Middle Eastern countries. In Syria, we eat stuffed (grape vine) leaves as a cold mezze.

The word yalanji, as we call it in Syria, is borrowed from Turkish and means "liar." There are two traditional fillings, one with meat, and another without. The meatless filling is the "liar," an impostor. In my recipe, I use chard leaves and pomegranate molasses for a sweet-sour taste.

Yalanji
— Swiss Chard Rolls with Rice Filling

First make the filling. In a large pot, fry the onion in the olive oil for 3 minutes. Add the rice and measured water and bring to a boil. Lower the heat, cover, and simmer for 8 minutes. Add the chopped tomatoes, parsley, mint, pomegranate molasses, and lemon juice. Cook everything for another 2 minutes. Add salt and pepper to taste.

Fill a bowl with iced water. Bring a large pot of water to a boil. Carefully submerge the chard leaves in the boiling water, and boil for 2 minutes Skim the leaves out of the water, cool them in the bowl of iced water, and then drain on paper towels.

Slice the chard leaves lengthwise and remove the hard middle stem. Place a small spoonful of filling on each half-leaf, fold the sides toward the inside, and roll up the yalanji like you would a spring roll. Repeat with the remaining leaves and filling.

Arrange a layer of potato slices on the bottom of a large, deep frying pan; this prevents the yalanji from sticking. Layer the tomato slices on top, and then the yalanji rolls, arranging them tightly so that they don't unroll during cooking.

Make the dressing. In a small bowl, mix the lemon juice, pomegranate molasses, olive oil, and measured water. Add salt and pepper to taste. Pour the dressing over the yalanji. Add enough water to just barely cover the yalanji. Set a small plate on top of them in the pot to keep them in place while cooking.

Cover, bring to a simmer, and cook for about 1 hour on low heat, until almost all of the liquid has been absorbed. Remove from the heat and cool, covered, until the remaining liquid is absorbed. Serve as a cold mezze or as a showstopper vegetarian main dish.

MAKES 40

Ice cubes (for iced water)
20 Swiss chard leaves

FOR THE FILLING
1 large white onion (chopped)
Scant ½ cup (100 ml) of extra-virgin olive oil
½ cup (100 g) of long-grain white rice
 (rinsed and soaked in water for
 about 10 minutes)
Generous ¾ cup (200 ml) of water
5 tomatoes (chopped)
1 large bunch of flat-leaf parsley (finely chopped)
2 teaspoons of dried mint
2 tablespoons of pomegranate molasses
Juice of 1 organic lemon
Salt and pepper

FOR COOKING
2 potatoes (cut into slices
 about ½ inch/1 cm thick)
3 tomatoes (thickly sliced)

FOR THE DRESSING
Juice of 1 organic lemon
1 tablespoon of pomegranate molasses
3½ tablespoons of extra-virgin olive oil
1 cup (250 ml) of water
Salt and pepper

Biwaz
— Simple Onion and Parsley Salad

PREPARATION

In a bowl, toss all the ingredients together using your fingers, making sure the parsley and onion slices are well coated with pomegranate molasses and sumac.

INGREDIENTS

SERVES 4

1 large bunch of flat-leaf parsley (coarsely chopped)
2 red onions (thinly sliced)
1 tablespoon of sumac
1 tablespoon of pomegranate molasses
2 tablespoons of extra-virgin olive oil
Salt

Biwaz is a simple salad of onions, parsley, and sumac. It is usually served with meat, adding texture and flavors to dishes like shawarma (see page 93), and it is a must with kebabs.

MEAT DISHES

There was always
someone outside,
brushing off the grill
and setting up the
lawn chairs.

Midsummer barbecues

—

Syrians love to barbecue and the summers of my youth were punctuated by evenings grilling food outside. There was always someone outside, brushing off the grill and setting up the lawn chairs. I remember barbecues held on farms, or on the garden lawns of family members or friends. Of course, we would have barbecues at home in our own backyard, too. In my memories, those evenings were always sunny; funny how memory works.

Barbecues always started at sunset—people were relaxed; the mood was leisurely and easygoing. We gathered to do more than just eat, after all. Someone would start the fire, chatting all the while, and the woman of the house would start marinating some extra meat. Aside from some halved onions, tomatoes, and roasted peppers, there were no vegetables on the grill; barbecues were not planned with vegetarians in mind.

All the mezze, salads, and other small side dishes were laid out on a long table. One end of the table was reserved for the children; the other end was for the oldest guests. Everyone would arrive with food to share: hummus bi tahini (page 60); biwaz (page 135); moutabal (page 48); and muhammara (page 83). After the guests arrived, the woman of the house sat down—from that moment on, cooking was men's business. The men would roast the meats over the barbecue and people would eat them right from the grill, as hot as possible. This was repeated until all the meat was gone. But even then, the party was far from over, and we would keep talking late into the night.

That is how I remember my summers in Syria: night after night of barbecues lined up, as if summer was one long skewer of outdoor celebration.

Sabankh bil roz
— Stew of Spinach and Ground Beef

PREPARATION

In a bowl, combine the ground beef, allspice, and a good pinch of salt and pepper. Knead until well combined. Form the mixture into meatballs that are about 2 inches (5 cm) in diameter. Set aside.

Heat the olive oil in a large pot over medium heat. Fry the onion and garlic for 3 minutes, until light golden. Sear the meatballs in batches, turning them regularly. Return all of the meatballs to the pot.

Add the spinach, stock, and a pinch of salt (to help the spinach wilt and cook). Cover and simmer for 2 minutes.

Add the ground allspice and salt and pepper to taste, stirring them in carefully so that the meatballs don't fall apart. The spinach will give off some moisture. Simmer the stew over medium heat for 5–7 minutes, until the liquid has reduced by half.

In a little bowl, whisk together all the ingredients for the lemon sauce.

Serve the stew warm, drizzled with the lemon sauce and accompanied by vermicelli rice.

INGREDIENTS

SERVES 4

FOR THE MEATBALLS
12 oz (350 g) of ground beef
Salt and pepper
2 tablespoons of ground allspice

FOR THE STEW
2 tablespoons of extra-virgin olive oil
1 onion (chopped)
3 garlic cloves (minced)
1 lb 12 oz (800 g) of baby spinach
 (washed and coarsely chopped)
⅔ cup (150 ml) of chicken or beef stock
1 tablespoon of ground allspice
Salt and pepper

FOR THE LEMON SAUCE
1 shallot or scallion (finely chopped)
Juice of 1 organic lemon
2 tablespoons of white or apple cider vinegar
½ teaspoon of crushed red pepper flakes

Syrian cuisine has several popular stews, or yakhni, and this spinach stew with meatballs is one of them. It is not the most elegant of dishes to look at, and, as a kid, I didn't want to eat it for this reason. I changed my mind when my mother reminded me about spinach-eating Popeye and his bulging muscles. Now I think it's delicious as well as nutritious! The lemon sauce goes well with it, and my mother always served it this way, though she actually borrowed the use of lemon sauce from another dish.

MEAT DISHES   (143)

Just like sabankh bil roz (see page 142), this hearty beef stew is also a yakhni, and is served with rice in the Syrian style. It wouldn't be the first choice for a dinner party; it is usually eaten in close family settings. If you do happen to find yourself sitting at a table where it is being served, consider it a compliment because the message is clear: you're part of the family.

Bazela bil roz
— Beef Stew with Green Peas

Heat the oil in a large pot and sear the meat on all sides until golden brown and caramelized. Remove the meat from the pan and set aside.

Fry the onion, carrot, and a'atryaat for 5 minutes in the same pot. Return the meat to the pot, along with the tomato paste and paprika, and continue to cook for another minute.

Add the tomato juice, 2 cups (500 ml) of water, and a good pinch of salt and pepper. Bring to a boil and then turn the heat down to low. Cover and simmer for 1 hour, until the meat is tender. Add a bit more water if the cooking liquid evaporates too quickly.

Remove and discard the a'atryaat. Add the peas and the pomegranate molasses and continue to simmer until the peas are cooked. Taste and add more salt and pepper, if needed.

Serve the stew immediately, accompanied by vermicelli rice.

INGREDIENTS

SERVES 6

4 tablespoons of extra-virgin olive oil

1 lb 2 oz (500 g) of stewing beef
  (cut into 1½-inch/4 cm pieces)

2 large onions (chopped)

2 carrots (cut into pieces)

1 a'atryaat (2 cinnamon sticks, 2 cloves,
  3 green cardamom pods, and 1 bay leaf
  tied in a bundle, see page 16)

2 tablespoons of tomato paste

1 tablespoon of paprika

3½ cups (800 ml) of tomato juice

Salt and pepper

3½ cups (500 g) of frozen peas

2 tablespoons of pomegranate molasses

Mnazaleh batinjan
— Baked Eggplants and Ground Beef in Tomato Sauce

PREPARATION

Preheat the oven to 425°F (220°C).

Rub the eggplant slices with 2 tablespoons of olive oil and place on a baking sheet lined with parchment paper. Season with salt and pepper and bake for 20 minutes until they are somewhat tender.

In the meantime, heat the other tablespoon of oil in a nonstick pan over medium heat. Fry the onion for 3 minutes. Add the beef, and brown it while breaking it into little pieces with a wooden spoon. Mix in the pine nuts, 7 spices blend, and some salt.

In a measuring cup, mix the tomato paste and the passata with the boiling water. Add salt and pepper and set aside.

Grease an 8 x 12 inch (20 x 30 cm) baking dish. Place a layer of eggplant slices in the base, reserving a few slices for the top, and then simply fill it with the rest of the vegetables, in no particular order.

Distribute the ground beef on top of and around the vegetables. Pour the tomato sauce over the whole dish and then top with the reserved eggplant slices.

Cover well with aluminum foil and bake for 30 minutes. Remove the foil and place the dish under the broiler for 10 minutes, until the top has caramelized. Garnish with toasted pine nuts and serve with rice.

———

*The eggplants are traditionally cut into strips for this dish so that you can see the mix of white flesh and purple skin. It reminds me of the ablaq architecture so typical of Syria, of which precious little now remains.

INGREDIENTS

SERVES 6

2 eggplants (cut into rounds about ½ inch/1 cm thick)*
3 tablespoons of extra-virgin olive oil
Salt and pepper
1 onion (finely chopped)
14 oz (400 g) of ground beef
3 tablespoons of pine nuts (toasted), plus extra to garnish
1 tablespoon of 7 spices blend (see page 15)
3 tablespoons of tomato paste
⅔ cup (150 ml) of tomato passata or purée
1½ cups (350 ml) of boiling water
2 tomatoes (sliced)
1 large onion (sliced into rings)
2 green peppers (sliced into rings)

TO SERVE
Steamed rice

This baked dish has a special place in my heart. It was the last meal I shared with my father a few weeks before he passed away. Of all the recipes in my mother's repertoire, this was his favorite. To be honest, all the recipes my mother makes with tomato sauce are amazing. She cooks her tomatoes slow, slow, slow—until the flavors are concentrated and rich.

This important Syrian recipe is called "upside down," since it is served upside down. There is certain to be a bit of anticipatory panic, at least in my family, because you only get one chance to turn it out of the pan. It is a stressful moment placing the plate over the pan, and turning the whole thing over. You just have to hope for the best! But it is delicious however it comes out. Traditionally old forks and knives were placed on the bottom to ensure that the eggplant would easily come loose. Makloube is also eaten in Jordan and Palestine, where other vegetables such as cauliflower are used.

Makloube
— Eggplant and Beef Pilaf

Heat 2 tablespoons of the olive oil in a large pot over high heat. Brown the lamb on all sides.

Add 4¼ cups (1 liter) of water, the onion, and the a'atryaat. Bring to a boil and then turn the heat down to low, cover, and simmer for an hour. Add some more water if needed.

Preheat the oven to 425°F (220°C).

While the lamb is cooking, line a baking sheet with parchment paper. Place the eggplant slices on the lined pan and brush them with the remaining olive oil. Generously season with salt and pepper, and bake for 30 minutes, flipping the slices over halfway through. Set aside.

When the lamb is cooked, remove it from the cooking liquid. Mix 1 teaspoon of the allspice into the stock, taste, and add more salt and pepper if desired. Set aside.

In a saucepan, brown the ground beef over medium heat, breaking it apart with a wooden spoon. Add the remaining ½ teaspoon of allspice, and a good pinch of salt and pepper, and continue stirring until all the liquid has evaporated.

Now assemble the makloube: arrange the eggplant slices over the base of a large baking dish or roasting pan. Start by arranging the slices so they meet in the center, and work outwards towards the edges of the pan, overlapping them slightly. There should not be any spaces where the rice filling could show through.

Spoon the rice onto the eggplant, followed by a layer of lamb and about two-thirds of the browned ground beef. Set aside the rest of the ground beef for a

SERVES 8

6 tablespoons of extra-virgin olive oil
9 oz (250 g) of lamb shoulder (cubed)
1 onion (quartered)
1 a'atryaat (2 cinnamon sticks, 2 cloves,
  3 green cardamom pods, and 1 bay leaf
  tied in a bundle, see page 16)
4 eggplants (cut into lengthwise
  slices, ½ inch/1 cm thick)
Salt and pepper
1½ teaspoons of ground allspice
10½ oz (300 g) of ground beef
2 cups (400 g) of long-grain white rice
  (rinsed and soaked for 10 minutes)

TO SERVE
⅓ cup (50 g) of pine nuts (toasted)
⅓ cup (50 g) of blanched almonds (toasted)

garnish. Pour 2 cups (500 ml) of the reserved stock onto the rice and meat. The rice must be completely covered. Cover the dish or pan with a double layer of aluminum foil and bake for 25 minutes, or until the rice is tender.

Take the makloube out of the oven and set aside to cool for 45 minutes. Then, when you are ready to serve, select a flat serving plate larger than the diameter of your baking dish or pan. Place it face-down on top of the makloube. Hold onto both the plate and baking dish or pan securely and flip the makloube onto the plate. Carefully remove the baking dish or pan.

Arrange the rest of the ground beef around the makloube. Garnish with pine nuts and almonds.

Lahme bi sayniyi
— Lamb Koftas in Tahini Sauce

Preheat the oven to 400°F (200°C).

In a large bowl, knead all the kofta ingredients together for 3 minutes until smooth (this may also be done in a food processor).

Spread the seasoned meat evenly over the bottom of a round baking dish or pan. Press it into a compact layer.

Arrange the tomato slices and green chili peppers over the meat.

Bake for 20 minutes in the middle of the oven, until the juices are released and the meat is almost completely cooked. Remove from the oven and carefully pour the meat juices into a small saucepan.

Add the tahini, lemon juice, and pomegranate molasses to the meat juices in the saucepan. Whisk this mixture for 5 minutes over high heat until the sauce boils.

Pour the sauce over the kofta. Turn on your broiler and broil the kofta for 10–15 minutes, until the tomatoes and peppers start to char.

Serve the dish warm, accompanied by spicy potatoes or bread.

SERVES 4

FOR THE KOFTA
12 oz (350 g) of ground lamb
12 oz (350 g) of ground beef
2 large onions (grated)
1 bunch of flat-leaf parsley (finely chopped)
1 tablespoon of ground coriander
1 tablespoon of ground allspice
1 tablespoon of paprika
1 tomato (grated, reserving the juice)
Salt and pepper to taste

FOR COOKING
4 tomatoes (thinly sliced)
2 mild green chili peppers (sliced in half or into rings)

FOR THE SAUCE
4 tablespoons of tahini
Juice of 1 organic lemon
1 tablespoon of pomegranate molasses

My mother often made this kofta during a time when we used to host family dinners for upwards of thirty people. Ground meat—better if it wasn't too lean—was ordered from the butcher. An enormous dish of meat topped with tomato slices was brought to the ferran, the community oven. This was the only oven big enough for the pan my mother used. She served her kofta with French fries or spicy potatoes (page 56), though they are good with flatbread, too.

Kibbeh

If hummus (pages 60 and 61) is the king of the Syrian table, then kibbeh is the undisputed queen. Kibbeh goes by various names: kubbeh, kibi, kobbah, kbaybi, and so on. And, as if that were not confusing enough, there are also many ways to prepare kibbeh—at least twenty. But no matter which way you make it, bulgur and meat (either beef or lamb) are two typical ingredients. Their popularity is undisputed: these deep-fried kibbeh balls are everyone's favorite warm mezze. My variation (see page 156) is reminiscent of croquettes, with its crispy outside and meat filling.

My grandmother used to hold a kibbeh cooking party once a year. Various other female family members were invited to make kibbeh with an expert—a woman who knew everything there was to know about kibbeh. The goal for that day was to make enough kibbeh to freeze for later. The meat and the coarse bulgur were to be mashed in a big mortar and then kneaded by hand into a meat pâté. Nowadays food processors and blenders make quick work of this tedious part of the preparation. No more kibbeh midwives are needed.

Kibbeh
— Bulgur and Meat Croquettes

PREPARATION

MAKE THE FILLING
In a large saucepan, heat the oil over medium heat. Fry the onion for 3 minutes, and then add the ground beef, breaking it into small pieces with a wooden spoon. Brown for 5–6 minutes, until cooked and all the liquid has evaporated. Mix in the pine nuts and pomegranate molasses. Add the 7 spices blend and salt. Fry for another 2 minutes and then cool.

MAKE THE DOUGH
In a large bowl, mix the bulgur, cayenne pepper, cumin, allspice, and a pinch of salt. Add the boiling water and let the bulgur stand for 5 minutes to absorb the water.

While the bulgur is soaking, combine the ground beef, ice, and ½ tablespoon of salt in a food processor and process to a smooth paste.

Transfer the meat paste to a bowl and add the grated onion, with its juice, and the bulgur. Knead for 2–3 minutes until it forms a homogeneous, pliable dough. If the dough feels too stiff, add a few tablespoons of water to give it a smooth and supple consistency.

MAKE THE CROQUETTES
Divide the dough into 15–20 balls, each about 1¼ inches (3 cm) in diameter.

Wet your hands and, using your finger, make a depression in one ball. Gradually shape the ball into a small oval, being careful to not tear the dough. Place a teaspoon of the filling in the middle of the oval and fold the edges over the center. Press the seams together so that the kibbeh is smooth and compact. Repeat with the remaining balls of dough.

INGREDIENTS

MAKES 15–20

FOR THE FILLING	FOR THE DOUGH
1 tablespoon of extra-virgin olive oil	7 oz (200 g) of extra-fine bulgur*
2 onions (chopped)	1 tablespoon of cayenne pepper
9 oz (250 g) of ground beef	½ teaspoon of ground cumin
3 tablespoons of pine nuts (toasted)	1 teaspoon of ground allspice
2 tablespoons of pomegranate molasses	Salt
1 tablespoon of 7 spices blend (see page 15)	1 cup (250 ml) of boiling water
½ teaspoon of salt	7 oz (200 g) of ground beef
	1½ oz (40 g) of ice (cubes or crushed)
Vegetable oil for frying	1 large onion (grated, reserving the juice)
Organic lemon (quartered) for serving	
—	
Food processor	

In a large pot, pour in the oil to a depth of about 2 inches (5 cm) and heat to 350°F (180°C). If you don't have a kitchen thermometer, test-fry one of the kibbeh; the oil should start to bubble around it as soon as it hits the oil.

Working in batches, deep-fry the kibbeh for 5 minutes or so, until crisp and brown. Using a slotted spoon, transfer to a plate lined with paper towels to drain. Serve the kibbeh warm or at room temperature, accompanied by lemon slices.

———

*If you cannot find extra-fine bulgur, grind up coarse bulgur in a spice grinder or food processor until it has a fine, sandy texture.

Every city has its own special kibbeh recipe and every family has its own special way of making it. This recipe is based on one from Aleppo and, though my mother hardly cooks any Aleppian food, this way of making kibbeh—served with a tomato-pomegranate sauce—is her favorite. She tweaked the standard Aleppian recipe by omitting the extra pieces of meat that usually would be in the ground beef and adds a lot of extra onion. Do what I do and serve kibbeh with rice; it's a meal all unto itself!

Kibbeh hamoud
— Kibbeh in Sour Tomato–Pomegranate Sauce

In a large pot, heat the olive oil over medium heat and fry the onion, garlic, and cilantro for 5 minutes. Push the onion mixture to the side of the pot. Add the tomato paste to the middle of the pot and fry for 1 minute before mixing it into the onion mixture.

Stir in the pomegranate juice, tomato juice, and a generous ¾ cup (200 ml) of water. Then add the pomegranate molasses, butter, dried mint, and some salt and pepper and bring the sauce to a boil. Immediately lower the heat and simmer the sauce for 30 minutes, until somewhat reduced.

Stir in the lemon juice, then carefully place the kibbeh in the sauce. Cover and simmer for 5–10 minutes, or until the kibbeh are warmed through.

Serve the kibbeh hamoud in bowls, garnished with a sprinkling of fresh parsley and pomegranate seeds.

———

*If you cannot find any pomegranate juice free of sugar or other additives, you can make your own fresh juice by blending fresh pomegranate seeds in the blender and then straining the juice through a fine sieve.

SERVES 4

1 quantity kibbeh (page 156)
4 tablespoons of extra-virgin olive oil
2 onions (sliced in thin rings)
3 garlic cloves (pressed)
1 bunch of cilantro (coarsely chopped)
2 tablespoons of tomato paste
2 cups (450 ml) of pure pomegranate juice
  (with no added sugar)*
2 cups (450 ml) of tomato juice
4 tablespoons of pomegranate molasses
3½ tablespoons (50 g) of butter
1 tablespoon of dried mint
Salt and pepper
Juice of 1 organic lemon

TO SERVE
1 handful of flat-leaf parsley (coarsely chopped)
1 handful of pomegranate seeds

Kibbeh laban
— Kibbeh in Mint–Yogurt Sauce

PREPARATION

In a small dish, dissolve the cornstarch in
2 tablespoons of cold water.

In a large pot over medium heat, whisk
together the yogurt, buttermilk, dried mint, and
dissolved cornstarch until the yogurt begins to
bubble and thicken.

Slip the kibbeh into the yogurt sauce, stirring
carefully, until completely covered with the
thickened sauce. Add salt and pepper to taste and
cook over medium heat for 5–10 minutes until
the kibbeh are warmed through.

For the topping, heat the olive oil in a small nonstick
pan and fry the garlic for 2–3 minutes until
golden yellow, being careful not to let it burn.
Stir in the cilantro and fry for another 2 minutes.

Spoon the kibbeh laban onto a serving platter.
Drizzle liberally with the garlic and cilantro oil
and then sprinkle with toasted pine nuts.
Serve immediately, accompanied by rice.

INGREDIENTS

SERVES 4

1 quantity kibbeh (page 156)

FOR THE MINT–YOGURT SAUCE
2 tablespoons of cornstarch
2 cups (500 g) of Greek yogurt
1 cup (240 ml) of buttermilk
1 tablespoon of dried mint
Salt and pepper

TOPPINGS
Scant ½ cup (100 ml) of extra-virgin olive oil
6 garlic cloves (pressed)
1 bunch of cilantro (finely chopped)
3 tablespoons of pine nuts (toasted)

*It's hard to find good kibbeh outside of Syria, so all
Syrians share a sort of homesickness for it. In this
recipe, the kibbeh are served in a yogurt sauce.
The raw kibbeh are sometimes cooked directly in the
yogurt sauce, but I think it tastes better when they are
first deep-fried. The sauce's freshness complements
the crispiness nicely. Kibbeh toppings are an essential
component of kibbeh laban. Do not omit the fried garlic,
cilantro, and pine nuts!*

For this recipe, the kibbeh are split into three layers and baked in the oven. A filling of ground beef, onion, and nuts is sandwiched in between the two layers of the dough, which is made of ground beef and bulgur. My mother gets creative with her knife and makes a pretty pattern on top. This also helps with cutting portions after baking. The presentation is impressive and it's no surprise that it is a popular dish at parties. In our family, it is served with dips, such as eggplant moutabal (page 48) or beet moutabal (page 67).

Kibbeh sayniyi
— Kibbeh Tart

PREPARATION

MAKE THE FILLING
In a large saucepan, heat the oil on medium heat
and fry the onion for 3 minutes. Add the ground
beef as soon as the onion starts to soften, breaking
it up into pieces with a wooden spoon. Cook for
5–6 minutes until it is completely browned and the
moisture has evaporated.

Stir in the toasted pine nuts and the pomegranate
molasses with the ground beef. Add the 7 spices blend
and the salt. Fry for another 2 minutes and then cool.

MAKE THE DOUGH
In a large bowl, combine the bulgur, cayenne pepper,
cumin, allspice, and a pinch of salt. Add the boiling
water and let stand for 5 minutes until it is absorbed.

While the bulgur is soaking, make a smooth paste out
of the ground beef, ice, and a good pinch of salt in
the food processor.

Knead the meat paste and grated onion, including the
onion juice, and the soaked bulgur for 2–3 minutes,
until it forms a homogeneous, pliable dough. If the
dough feels too stiff, add a couple of tablespoons
of water to give it a smooth and supple consistency.

Weigh the dough and divide into two equal portions.

Preheat the oven to 400°F (200°C).

MAKE THE TART
Grease a 12 inch (30 cm) tart pan with half of the
melted butter. Spread half of the kibbeh dough over
the bottom in a layer about ½ inch (1 cm) thick.

Spread the meat filling over the dough, leaving a
space of ½ inch (1 cm) around the entire perimeter.

INGREDIENTS

SERVES 10

FOR THE FILLING	FOR THE DOUGH
1 tablespoon of olive oil	14 oz (400 g) of extra-fine bulgur
2 onions (chopped)	2 tablespoons of cayenne pepper
9 oz (250 g) of ground beef	1 teaspoon of ground cumin
3 tablespoons of pine nuts (toasted)	2 tablespoons of ground allspice
2 tablespoons of pomegranate molasses	Salt
1 tablespoon of 7 spices blend (see page 15)	2 cups (500 ml) of boiling water
½ teaspoon of salt	14 oz (400 g) of ground beef
—	3 oz (80 g) of ice (about 3 cubes)
Food processor	2 large onions (grated, reserve the juice)
Round metal tart pan (12 inches/30 cm in diameter)	7 tablespoons (100 g) of butter, melted

This allows for the two dough layers to be pressed
against each other to form a nice crust edge. Gently
press the filling into the dough. Spread the second
half of the dough in a layer about ½ inch (1 cm) thick
over the filling. Firmly press the layer on top of the
whole tart, making sure there are no gaps in the
dough at the edge.

Brush the top dough layer with the remaining half of
the melted butter. Using a thin, sharp knife, cut
decorative strips in the top of the tart dough.

Set the tart pan in the middle of the oven and bake for
40 minutes, until golden brown. Cut the kibbeh into
6 slices, like a pizza, and then cut each slice diagonally
to form smaller diamond shapes (see photo).

(165)

Mahshi el jazar
— Stuffed Parsnips in Tomato Sauce

PREPARATION

Use a corer or melon baller to hollow out the parsnips, leaving room to eventually stuff them. Be careful not to break through the outside, and do not pierce through the other end of the parsnip.

In a large bowl, mix the rice, ground beef, allspice, and mint. Add salt and pepper to taste.

Fill the parsnips with the beef and rice mixture, but do not overfill because the rice will swell during cooking.

Melt the butter in a deep pot and cook the garlic for a couple of minutes. Add the chopped tomatoes, orange juice, passata, pomegranate molasses, and mint. Stir in the measured water.

Carefully arrange the parsnips in the sauce. Bring to a boil, and then turn the heat to low and simmer for 1 hour, or until the parsnips are tender and the rice is cooked. Add salt and pepper to taste.

INGREDIENTS

SERVES 6

2 lb 4 oz (1 kg) of peeled parsnips
   (preferably not too small)
Salt and pepper

FOR THE FILLING
Scant ½ cup (75 g) of long-grain white rice
   (rinsed and soaked for 10 minutes)
5½ oz (150 g) of ground beef
2 tablespoons of ground allspice
1 teaspoon of dried mint

FOR THE SAUCE
3½ tablespoons (50 g) of butter
4 garlic cloves (minced)
14 oz (400 g) can of chopped tomatoes
Juice of 1 orange
1¼ cups (300 ml) of tomato passata or purée
1 tablespoon of pomegranate molasses
3 teaspoons of dried mint
1 cup (250 ml) of lukewarm water
—
Apple or vegetable corer or melon baller

Not every Syrian will be familiar with this recipe; it is a local specialty from Homs, where my family is from. The name means "stuffed carrots" even though the carrot traditionally used is actually a cross between a carrot and a parsnip. It only grows regionally and is impossible to find outside of Homs. When we lived in Saudi Arabia, my grandmother would fill packages with kilos of jazar every winter and send them to us. I don't need to tell you how important this dish is for our family recipe collection!

Shorbat ameh
— Tomato Soup with Barley and Lamb Shanks

Heat the oil in a large pot over high heat and brown the lamb shanks (two at a time) until they are fully seared and caramelized. Nicely caramelized meat does not stick to the bottom of the pot when turning.

Place the lamb shanks on a plate and set aside. In the same pot, sauté the onions with the garlic, a'atryaat, tomato paste, cayenne pepper, and cumin, until the onions are soft and translucent. Return the lamb shanks to the pot and stir to coat the lamb with the onion mixture. Add the water, tomato juice, and a generous sprinkling of salt and pepper, and bring to a boil. Immediately turn the heat to low, cover, and simmer for 2 hours, or until the lamb is cooked, skimming the foam from time to time if necessary.

Remove the a'atryaat from the soup and discard. Add the pearl barley and cook for another 20 minutes, until tender. Taste and add salt and pepper.

Sprinkle the soup with with chopped cilantro, if desired, and serve with lemon wedges.

INGREDIENTS

SERVES 6

3 tablespoons of extra-virgin olive oil
4 lamb shanks
2 onions (coarsely chopped)
3 garlic cloves (minced)
1 a'atryaat (2 cinnamon sticks, 2 cloves,
  3 green cardamom pods, and 1 bay
  leaf tied in a bundle, see page 16)
3 tablespoons of tomato paste
1 tablespoon of cayenne pepper
½ teaspoon of ground cumin
8½ cups (2 liters) of lukewarm water
4¼ cups (1 liter) of tomato juice
Salt and pepper
1 cup (200 g) of pearl barley

TO SERVE
1 bunch of cilantro (coarsely chopped, optional)
1 organic lemon (cut into wedges)

Just like all of the other soups in this book, Syrian households often serve this soup as part of the Ramadan table. Traditionally, it is made with good-quality cuts of boneless lamb. Lamb shanks are known as "bananas" in Syria. Nowadays, I don't cut the meat from the bone, but rather cook the whole "banana" in the soup. This makes the soup even easier to prepare, and just that much tastier!

Ouzi
— Filo Pastries with Meat and Rice Filling

Heat the oil in a large pot over medium heat. Brown the meat for 7 minutes, breaking it up into small pieces with a wooden spoon. Stir in the 7 spices blend.

Mix in the rice and cardamom and add the beef stock. Add a pinch of salt and pepper, and continue cooking the rice for 15 minutes, or until most of the stock has been absorbed.

Stir the peas and the toasted nuts into the cooked rice. Warm everything for another minute and then turn the heat off, cover, and let the pilaf rest for 5 minutes. Add salt and pepper to taste.

Make the pastries using a little bowl or cup (3½ inches/9 cm in diameter): Stack two sheets of filo dough, fold them in half, and brush them with some olive oil to help them stick together. Line the little bowl or cup with this double layer of filo to form a filo cup, leaving some of the sheets hanging over the edge.

Fill the filo cup with the pilaf and press on the rice using the round part of a spoon. Fold the overhanging filo over the rice to cover. Seal the filo edges by brushing once more with some olive oil. Turn the pastry out onto a plate. Repeat to form the rest of the pastries in the same way.

Preheat the oven to 400°F (200°C). Line a baking sheet with parchment paper. Set the pastries on the parchment paper and then brush them with olive oil. Bake for 15–20 minutes, until they are a nice golden brown. Garnish each pastry with a pistachio before serving them warm.

INGREDIENTS

MAKES 10

2 tablespoons of extra-virgin olive oil
1 lb 2 oz (500 g) of ground beef
1 tablespoon of 7 spices blend
  (see page 15)
Generous ½ cup (100 g) of long-grain
  white rice (rinsed)
½ teaspoon of ground cardamom
2 cups (500 ml) of beef stock
Salt and pepper
1⅓ cups (200 g) of frozen peas
⅔ cup (100 g) of toasted nuts
  (almonds, cashews, pine nuts)
20 sheets of filo dough
  (each 8 x 10 inches/20 x 25 cm)
Olive oil for brushing

TO SERVE
Handful of pistachios

These hearty and comforting pastries are typical of Damascus. They are beautiful to present and make an impression on your dinner table. Every guest is served their own small, savory ouzi, as though made especially with them in mind. As a child, I ate these often when we were invited to my parents' friends' house. They came from the capital city and I was always excited to visit them, wondering: will they serve ouzi pastries again?

Kebab karaz
— Lamb Kebabs with Cherries

PREPARATION

In a large bowl, knead the ground lamb, onion, allspice, salt, and pepper with the palm of your hand until well mixed. Cover and refrigerate for 30 minutes. This will make it easier to form meatballs from the mixture.

While the mixture is in the refrigerator, heat a pot over medium heat and add the cherries, water, pomegranate molasses, cinnamon, and lemon juice. Add salt and pepper to taste. Bring the mixture to a boil and then turn the heat to low. Simmer the sauce for 20 minutes, stirring occasionally, until the cherries are soft. Mash some of the cherries to release their juices and flavor.

Remove the meat mixture from the refrigerator. To test if it is well seasoned, brown a small amount, and then taste and add more salt, pepper, or spices to the remaining mixture as necessary. Form the remaining mixture into meatballs measuring ¾ inch (2 cm) in diameter.

In a large nonstick frying pan, heat the olive oil over high heat and, working in batches if necessary, brown the meatballs for 2 minutes, turning regularly to sear evenly.

Spoon the meatballs and their juices into the pot of cherry sauce. Simmer for another 10 minutes.

Sprinkle the dish with toasted pine nuts and chopped mint. Serve warm with flatbread.

INGREDIENTS

SERVES 4

1 lb 2 oz (500 g) of ground lamb
1 large onion (chopped)
2 tablespoons of ground allspice
Salt and pepper
1 lb 2 oz (500 g) of cherries (pitted and halved)
1 cup (250 ml) of room temperature water
2 tablespoons of pomegranate molasses
1 teaspoon of cinnamon
Juice of 1 organic lemon
1 tablespoon of extra-virgin olive oil

TO SERVE
3½ tablespoons of pine nuts (toasted)
1 bunch of fresh mint (chopped)
Middle Eastern flatbread

This unusual kebab comes from Aleppo, which is located on the former Silk Road, the ancient merchant route connecting China, Central Asia, and the Middle East. This might explain why recipes from Aleppo are somewhat more exciting and richer in spices than the recipes from other parts of Syria, and this is true of this dish. The cherries make it a seasonal dish, a true summer treat.

Lamb and vegetable kebabs with khebzeh hamra

PREPARATION

In a bowl, knead all the kebab ingredients by hand until everything is mixed evenly. To test the flavors, brown a little of the mixture in a frying pan, taste, and add more spices to the remaining raw mixture as needed. Cover the mixture and refrigerate for at least 1 hour.

With moistened hands to keep the meat from sticking, divide the ground lamb into 6 balls of equal size. Form each ball into a flat kebab by rolling it around a skewer. Refrigerate the kebabs until ready to cook.

Heat your broiler or barbecue.

To make the vegetable kebabs, skewer the vegetables in whatever order you wish.

Broil or grill the meat and vegetable kebabs for 5 minutes on each side, or until cooked to your liking.

Brush the flatbreads with a spoonful of red pepper or tomato paste, cut them into quarters, and serve them with the kebabs. They are also delicious with biwaz (see page 135).

INGREDIENTS

SERVES 6

FOR THE KEBABS
1 lb 2 oz (500 g) of ground lamb
3 garlic cloves (minced)
1 bunch of flat-leaf parsley (finely chopped)
1 teaspoon of paprika
1 teaspoon of ground allspice
1 teaspoon of ground black pepper
½ teaspoon of ground nutmeg
½ teaspoon of salt, or to taste

FOR THE VEGETABLE KEBABS
4 red onions (quartered)
3 green peppers (cut into large pieces)
1 lb 2 oz (500 g) of tomatoes (halved)

FOR THE KHEBZEH HAMRA
6 Middle Eastern flatbreads
6 tablespoons of red pepper paste
  or tomato paste
—
12 flat metal skewers

This dish reminds me of summer, and of barbecues with friends and family in the backyard (see page 139). The seasoning is simple—a few mild spices and some parsley—so choose the best quality ground lamb you can find. The flavor of the meat will determine the flavor of the kebabs. The grilled vegetables go hand-in-hand with lamb kebabs. You won't find lamb kebabs without vegetables; they taste better together. An open (charcoal) fire gives the most flavorful result, but you can also simply broil the kebabs in the oven.

MEAT DISHES

CHICKEN
AND FISH DISHES

If we felt like eating fish, we would get in the car and go to the seaside, to a small town in Tartus, Bsireh, about an hour-and-a-half drive from Homs.

The table overlooking the sea
—

If we felt like eating fish, we would get in the car and go to the seaside,
to a small town in Tartus, Bsireh, about an hour-and-a-half drive from
Homs. My grandfather has a one-bedroom vacation house there, right on
the beach. My mother and her siblings spent their summers there when
they were young. They used to sleep on the sofas in the living room. Later
on, when grandchildren came along, there were days when up to twenty
people would spend the night in that little house. It still only had one
bedroom, so there was no place where there wasn't someone sleeping.
It was precisely this camaraderie in chaos that made the summers at my
grandfather's vacation house such an experience.

There wasn't too much going on in Bsireh. It was a low-key place with a
few shops and a seafood restaurant called the Green Coast. The restaurant
was a ten-minute walk along the beach from the vacation house. Mostly
locals ate there. We would go there to eat fish and for the view out towards
the sea. My grandparents had eaten there so often over the years that they
had a special table reserved with my grandmother's name. It was a choice
table with a panoramic view. No glass windowpane was needed because it
was never cold.

The fish served there smelled only of the sea. It was fresher than fresh and
was prepared without further ado. In all those years, I never saw a menu at
the Green Coast. The oldest man at the table—usually my grandfather—
would just order fish for everyone. While we waited, we would get a
mezze of seafood or fish; desserts were baskets of fruit or sweets. It all
tasted amazing, but not necessarily because of the cook's accomplishments.
No, it was the surroundings, the service, and the hospitality—not to
mention the vistas of the sea—that made the seafood dinners in Bsireh
so unforgettable.

(180)

Jambari ma'ala
— Shrimp with Garlic, Cilantro, and Cayenne Pepper

Heat the oil in a large nonstick frying pan and sauté the garlic with the cilantro for 3–4 minutes.

Add the shrimp, cayenne pepper, and lemon juice, and stir until the shrimp are coated evenly. Continue shaking the pan over the heat for about 5 minutes, until the shrimp are pink and cooked.

Add salt and pepper to taste. Serve immediately, with rice and salad.

SERVES 4

3 tablespoons of extra-virgin olive oil

5 garlic cloves (thinly sliced)

1 bunch of cilantro (finely chopped)

1 lb 2 oz (500 g) of jumbo shrimp (not peeled)

½ teaspoon of cayenne pepper

Juice of 1 organic lemon

Salt and pepper

These shrimp are often included on a tray of warm mezze, along with other small fish or seafood dishes. They are incredibly simple to make and, though the ingredients are completely ordinary, the results are something special. When I make this dish, I taste in the garlic and cilantro a powerful and evocative mixture of Mediterranean and Syrian flavors.

Tajen samak
— Fish with Sumac–Tahini Sauce

PREPARATION

Preheat the oven to 300°F (150°C).

In a large saucepan, heat the olive oil over medium heat. Fry the onion rings for 3–5 minutes until they are soft. Season with 2 teaspoons of the sumac, and salt and pepper to taste.

Spread the fried onions over the bottom of a baking dish and set the fish on top of them. Drizzle some olive oil over the fish and sprinkle it with the remaining 2 teaspoons of sumac, and some salt and pepper. Bake for 15 minutes in the middle of the oven.

While the fish is baking, make the sauce: Whisk all the sauce ingredients together in a bowl, adjusting the amount of lemon juice, garlic, salt, and pepper to your liking. Transfer to a small saucepan and, whisking constantly, warm the sauce over medium heat until it boils. Remove from the heat.

Remove the fish from the oven, pour the sauce over the fish to completely cover it, and then bake for another 10–15 minutes until cooked through.

Garnish with chopped parsley, toasted pine nuts, and sumac, and serve with lemon wedges.

INGREDIENTS

SERVES 4

2 tablespoons of extra-virgin olive oil, plus extra for drizzling
3 onions (sliced into rings)
4 teaspoons of sumac
Salt and pepper
1 lb 9 oz (700 g) of white fish fillets

FOR THE SAUCE
⅔ cup (150 ml) of tahini
Juice of 1–2 organic lemons (as desired)
¾ cup (170 ml) of water
4–6 garlic cloves (as desired, pressed)
1 teaspoon of ground nutmeg
Salt and pepper

TO SERVE
1 small bunch of flat-leaf parsley (chopped)
Small handful of pine nuts (toasted)
Sumac
Organic lemon (cut into wedges)

Given that Syrian fish recipes are usually very simple, my friend Hadi (also a passionate cook), and I started experimenting. Instead of drenching the fried fish in tahini sauce, which is what is usually done in Syria, we use tahini in the preparation. It gives a totally different result, in flavor and in structure. We serve the dish with rice, which, though unusual, is delicious.

(186)

Aghabani tablecloths

—

It is not only the food on the plates that make a Syrian table so recognizable. There is a distinctly Syrian adornment lying beneath those plates. Aghabani tablecloths are colorful, hand-embroidered, and as beautiful as they are unique. They have been made in Syria for 150 years. Traditionally, they were made from white or saffron-colored silk, and embroidered with gold or silver motifs of flowers, leaves, boughs, and trees. The patterns are inspired by the flora in the region where they are made.

As the legend goes, the tablecloths were named for two families—the Aghas and the Banis—who first had the idea to embroider such tablecloths. Though historians surmise the Aghabani handiwork originated in Homs, the city where I was born, the industry eventually flourished in Damascus. The housewives of Douma, a suburb of Damascus, are known for their embroidery. The art was passed from mother to daughter, and today, every household has a special sewing machine that can replicate the embroidered patterns. When daughters marry, they get a machine of their own as a wedding gift, which they then take with them to their new house. The tablecloths are now made from cotton, instead of silk, and are often embroidered with synthetic thread.

The beautiful motifs have exotic names, and no two are the same: al-arisheh (pergola edge), erk al-zanbaq (lily vein), and al-lozeh al rqiqa (thin almond). Aghabani tablecloths have also changed with the times; modern-day designs include modern, abstract colors and patterns. Blocks of poplar wood are carved with the motif and then they are dipped in a special paint and stamped on the tablecloths as a guide for the embroidery. For most tablecloths, one stamp is chosen for the edge motif and a second is chosen for the central design. The women embroiderers from Douma patiently make detailed stamps with artwork that is colorful and lively.

I have collected about ten tablecloths over the years, some of which are on loan from my mother, grandmother, and aunts. Others I have had since I was a child. They are often sold to tourists and you can see them piled up in the markets in tall, glittering stacks. But they are beautiful in my eyes. It doesn't get any more traditional than this. Set the table with one of these and, in the blink of an eye, you transform a regular old meal into a Syrian feast.

Sayadiyah
— Spiced Fish Pilaf with Caramelized Onions

PREPARATION

In a large frying pan, heat 4 tablespoons of the olive oil over medium heat. Add the onion slices to the hot oil and cook for 15 minutes until caramelized. Do not have the heat set too high because onions can burn easily. Spoon the caramelized onions out of the pan and drain them on paper towels. Reserve half for the garnish.

In a blender, pulse the other half of the caramelized onions to a thick, dark-brown paste. Add the stock, ground cardamom, ground cumin, cinnamon, cloves, and turmeric to the blender, and blend until smooth. Add salt and pepper to taste and set aside— this broth will be used to cook the rice.

In a deep pot, heat the remaining 2 tablespoons of olive oil over medium heat and sear the fish on both sides.

Add the rice to the cod in the pot. Pour the onion broth over the fish and rice and bring to a boil. Turn the heat down to low, cover, and simmer for 12–15 minutes, until the rice has cooked and absorbed all of the liquid. Turn off the heat and let the rice rest, covered, for 10 minutes. It should be fluffy in texture and will have absorbed all of the flavors.

Spoon the pilaf into a serving dish, breaking up the fish if you like, sprinkle with toasted nuts, and garnish with the reserved caramelized onions.

INGREDIENTS

SERVES 6

6 tablespoons of extra-virgin olive oil
5 onions (halved and thinly sliced)
3 cups (700 ml) of fish or vegetable stock
½ teaspoon of ground cardamom
½ teaspoon of ground cumin
½ teaspoon of ground cinnamon
½ teaspoon of ground cloves
½ teaspoon of ground turmeric
Salt and pepper
1 lb 2 oz (500 g) of boneless skinless cod fillets
2 cups (400 g) of long-grain white rice
  (rinsed and soaked for 10 minutes)
2 tablespoons of sliced almonds (toasted)
2 tablespoons of pine nuts (toasted)
—
Blender or food processor

To make traditional fish pilaf, you usually cook the rice and fish separately, and serve the fish on top of a mountain of rice. In my version, I cook the rice and fish in the same pot. This gives the flavors a chance to meld together. The juices from the cooking fish lend a creaminess to the rice. Other varieties of fish will work in this recipe, but choose a firm white fish that won't fall apart too easily while cooking.

You won't see this chicken kebab as often as you might come across other kebab and
meat dishes, such as shish tawook (page 194), and lamb and vegetable kebabs with
khebzeh hamra (page 174). But this recipe is definitely worth trying. I like to make it
with chicken thighs because they are more flavorful and juicy than chicken breasts. If
possible, let the chicken mixture marinate overnight to give the flavors time to develop.

Chicken kofta kebabs

PREPARATION

Combine all of the kebab ingredients in a food processor and pulse to combine. Blend on the regular setting for 1–2 minutes, until you have a smooth paste. Transfer the mixture to a bowl and cover with plastic wrap. Refrigerate for at least 2 hours, or overnight. This makes it easier to form the meat around the skewers. It also brings out the flavors in the chicken.

Preheat a barbecue or oven to 450°F (230°C).

Test to see if the ground chicken is well seasoned by frying a small portion to taste. That way you can decide if you would like to add any more spices or salt to the remaining raw mixture.

Take a big handful of the chicken mixture and, with moistened hands, form it around a skewer into a sausage shape, about 6 inches (15 cm) long, and 1½ inches (4 cm) thick. Repeat with the rest of the chicken mixture.

ON THE BARBECUE
Grill for 5 minutes on each side or until cooked through, golden brown, and slightly charred.

IN THE OVEN
Place the skewers on a baking sheet lined with parchment paper. Cover with aluminum foil and bake for 15 minutes. Turn on the broiler, remove the foil, and broil the skewers for 3–5 minutes on each side to recreate a barbecue effect.

The kebabs are delicious in flatbread, accompanied by fresh herbs and a squeeze of lemon juice.

INGREDIENTS

SERVES 4

14 oz (400 g) of boneless chicken thighs
   (cut into large pieces)
2 onions (peeled and quartered)
5 garlic cloves (peeled)
1 bunch of flat-leaf parsley (stems trimmed)
2 tablespoons of tomato paste
1 tablespoon of paprika
1 tablespoon of crushed red pepper flakes
2 tablespoons (30 g) of butter
Pinch of sal and pepper

TO SERVE (OPTIONAL)
Flatbread
Fresh herbs
Lemon halves (for squeezing)
Grilled onions
Toum (Middle Eastern aioli)
—
Food processor
Skewers

Shish tawook
— Chicken Shish Kebabs

In a sealable freezer bag, combine all of the ingredients except the honey. Seal the bag, toss the contents to blend them thoroughly, and rub the marinade into the chicken.

Place the bag on a plate or in a bowl (in case it leaks) and refrigerate for at least 3 hours.

Preheat a barbecue or oven to 450°F (230°C).

Thread the chicken pieces onto skewers, leaving 3 inches (8 cm) bare to use as a handle.

ON THE BARBECUE
Grill the skewers for 6–8 minutes, turning regularly, until the chicken is golden brown, slightly charred, and completely cooked. Drizzle with the honey and grill for a minute longer.

IN THE OVEN
Place the skewers on a baking sheet lined with parchment paper. Cover with aluminum foil (this keeps the chicken from drying out) and bake for 15 minutes. Turn on the broiler, remove the foil, drizzle the chicken with the honey, and then broil for 3 minutes on each side until charred and cooked through.

INGREDIENTS

SERVES 6

1 lb 12 oz (800 g) of boneless skinless
   chicken thighs (cut into 2 inch/5 cm pieces)
1⅔ cups (400 g) of Greek yogurt
4 tablespoons of tomato paste
6–8 garlic cloves (pressed)
Juice of 1 organic lemon
2 tablespoons of cayenne pepper
1 tablespoon of crushed red pepper flakes
1 tablespoon of ground cumin
4 tablespoons of extra-virgin olive oil
Pinch of salt
3½ tablespoons of honey

TO SERVE (OPTIONAL)
Lemon halves (for squeezing)
—
Skewers

Chicken kebabs are popular all over the world, and they are made countless ways. If you want to make chicken kebabs the Syrian way, you'll need garlic, lemon, paprika, and Aleppo pepper (see page 16), and I like to mix yogurt and tomato paste into the marinade also. Chicken thighs give a more succulent result than breasts. Finally, a drizzle of honey is a typical Syrian finish—it gives the kebabs a mouthwatering shine and a crispy sweet layer. These kebabs are delicious with toum (Middle Eastern garlic aioli). You can also serve them with flatbread and biwaz (see page 135).

This dish was originally cooked in a clay pot, hence the term "bi jara," or "from the clay oven" in the recipe's name. My version differs from the original, not only in that I have used a metal pot instead of a clay pot, but also because I have "dirtied" the bulgur by mixing it with vegetables and a lot of spices. A friend of mine inspired me with his dirty rice recipe. The chicken is marinated in the same Mediterranean seasonings that I later use for the bulgur—each reinforcing the other.

(196)

Red bulgur bi jara
— "Dirty" Bulgur with Roast Chicken

PREPARATION

Put the chicken in a sealable freezer bag with the olive oil, tomato paste, coriander, cayenne pepper, cumin, and a good pinch of salt and pepper. Seal the bag and rub all the marinade ingredients into the chicken. Marinate on a plate in the refrigerator for at least 2 hours or overnight.

Preheat the oven to 400°F (200°C).

Place the chicken in a baking dish. Pour the marinade over the chicken, cover with aluminum foil, and bake for 30 minutes, until cooked through. Turn on the broiler, remove the foil, and broil the chicken for another 10 minutes, until golden brown on top.

Meanwhile, pour the bulgur into a heatproof bowl and add boiling water to cover. Soak the bulgur for 5 minutes, then drain any excess water.

In a large pot, heat the olive oil over medium heat. Fry the shallots for 3 minutes until golden. Add the garlic and fry for another 2 minutes. Stir in the tomato paste, coriander, cayenne pepper, and cumin. Continue cooking until browned; this intensifies the flavors.

Add the chopped tomatoes, bulgur, and chicken stock. Season with salt and pepper to taste. Stir, cover, and simmer for 15 minutes, adding more water if necessary, until the bulgur is cooked.

Stir in the chickpeas and the peas. Warm the dish for a couple of minutes. Turn off the heat, cover, and let the dish rest for 5 minutes.

Spoon the bulgur into a serving dish, top with the chicken, and garnish liberally with fresh parsley.

INGREDIENTS

SERVES 4

FOR THE CHICKEN
4 whole chicken legs
1 tablespoon of extra-virgin olive oil
1 tablespoon of tomato paste
½ teaspoon of ground coriander
½ teaspoon of cayenne pepper
½ teaspoon of ground cumin
Salt and pepper

FOR THE BULGUR
1½ cups (200 g) of coarse bulgur
Boiling water
3 tablespoons of extra-virgin olive oil
4 French shallots (peeled and left whole)
2 garlic cloves (pressed)
1 tablespoon of tomato paste
1 teaspoon of ground coriander
1 teaspoon of cayenne pepper
½ teaspoon of ground cumin
14 oz (400 g) can of chopped tomatoes
Generous ¾ cup (200 ml) of chicken stock
Salt and pepper
Scant 1 cup (125 g) of canned or cooked chickpeas
Heaped 1 cup (150 g) of frozen peas

TO GARNISH
1 handful of flat-leaf parsley (chopped)

Summer salad
— Watermelon, Halloumi, and Mint Salad

PREPARATION

Heat a grill pan over medium heat and grill the
halloumi slices for 2 minutes on each side.

In a large bowl, toss the watermelon, grilled
halloumi, and pomegranate seeds with the olive oil
and 1 tablespoon of the pomegranate molasses.

Transfer the salad to a large serving dish, sprinkle
with mint leaves, and drizzle with the remaining
tablespoon of pomegranate molasses.

INGREDIENTS

SERVES 4

8 oz (225 g) of halloumi (cut into
  ½ inch/1 cm thick slices)
1 small watermelon (cut into pieces)
Seeds of 1 pomegranate
4 tablespoons of extra-virgin olive oil
2 tablespoons of pomegranate molasses
1 handful of fresh mint leaves

*Watermelon and salty white cheese are are often
served together as dessert in Syria. The combination
is delicious, and so I was inspired to create this simple
salad. It has a fresh summer taste and goes delightfully
with most chicken and fish dishes.*

Samke harra
— Fish in Spicy Nut Sauce

PREPARATION

Preheat the oven to 400°F (200°C).

Heat the oil in a large nonstick pan over medium heat. Fry the onions and garlic for 5 minutes, stirring constantly, until the onions begin to soften.

Add the tomatoes, hot red pepper paste, chili peppers, ground cumin, cayenne pepper, walnuts, lemon juice, and three-quarters of the chopped cilantro. Fry everything for 5 minutes. Taste and add more salt and pepper as desired.

Using a sharp knife, make diagonal cuts in the fish skin a few times, ¾ inch (2 cm) apart. Place both fish into a baking dish, slip some of the lemon slices into the cavity between the fish fillets, and spread the rest of the sauce and lemon slices around the fish. Rub the sauce into the diagonal cuts you made.

Bake for 20–30 minutes, until golden brown on top.

Top with remaining fresh cilantro and serve with rice or potatoes.

INGREDIENTS

SERVES 4

Scant ½ cup (100 ml) of extra-virgin olive oil
2 onions (coarsely chopped)
6 garlic cloves (thinly sliced)
2 large tomatoes (cubed)
2 tablespoons of spicy red pepper paste
2 red chili peppers (chopped)
2 teaspoons of ground cumin
2 teaspoons of cayenne pepper
Generous ¾ cup (100 g) of coarsely chopped walnuts
Juice of 1 organic lemon
1 large bunch of cilantro (coarsely chopped)
Salt and pepper
2 whole white fish (cleaned, gutted, and scaled)
1 organic lemon (thinly sliced)

In Syria, people eat fish primarily in the coastal regions and it is almost always prepared very simply. The fish is either grilled or fried without extra spices or seasonings. You eat it by dipping it in sauces like tarator (see page 21), or a sauce of olive oil, lemon, and garlic (see page 20). Very seldom is fish called for in a traditional Syrian recipe, though that is exactly what samke harra is!

Musakhan wraps
— Flatbread with Chicken, Onions, and Sumac

PREPARATION

Bring a large pot of water to a boil. Add the chicken breasts, a'atryaat, and a good pinch of salt and pepper. Boil the chicken for 20 minutes, until cooked through.

Drain the chicken breasts and cool. When they are cool enough to handle, shred the meat with your fingers.

In a pot, heat 3½ tablespoons (50 ml) of the olive oil over medium heat. Sauté the onions for 5 minutes, or until softened. Add the shredded chicken, sumac, pine nuts, and the remaining 3½ tablespoons (50 ml) of olive oil. Fry everything together for 5 minutes. Add salt and pepper to taste.

Place a few spoonfuls of the shredded chicken mixture onto each flatbread. Fold the sides of the flatbread toward the inside over the filling, and then fold into a rectangular parcel.

Heat a grill pan over high heat and cook the wraps for 2 minutes on each side until golden and crispy. Serve them warm with laban bi khyar.

INGREDIENTS

SERVES 6

3 boneless chicken breasts
1 a'atryaat (2 cinnamon sticks, 2 cloves,
  3 green cardamom pods, and 1 bay
  leaf tied in a bundle, see page 16)
Salt and pepper
Scant ½ cup (100 ml) of extra-virgin olive oil
5 large onions (coarsely chopped)
3 tablespoons of sumac
3 tablespoons of pine nuts (toasted)
6 flatbreads or tortillas
Laban bi khyar (page 80), to serve (optional)

This recipe is an ode to sumac—originally from Palestine, where they serve a whole chicken flavored with sumac on bread, topped with a whole lot of sumac-spiced onions. Using the same ingredients, I make a Syrian version by shredding the chicken, then frying it with onion and sumac and rolling it up in flatbread.

DESSERTS
AND BEVERAGES

Ramadan means
"being together,"
and this is how
I experience
Ramadan: surrounded
by the warm and
welcoming embrace
of family.

The Ramadan table
—

The non-Muslim world associates the holy month of Ramadan with fasting and privation. But Ramadan isn't about suffering; it is about empathy. Ramadan was a time of trying, at least in our family, to empathize with those less fortunate, and with people who don't have much, who don't know what it's like to have the luxury of a table laden with delicious food. It's also a time to leave bad habits behind: no more swearing, no lying, no more wasting money. Seen in this way, Ramadan is a time for simplicity, equality, and peace.

Spending time in the company of others is another aspect of Ramadan that is even more important for me personally. Ramadan means "being together," and this is how I experience Ramadan: surrounded by the warm and welcoming embrace of family. Daytime is the time for cooking, and for talking about what you are looking forward to eating later on that evening. After the sun sets (always at about six o'clock in the evening in Syria), you sit down with everyone around the table.

At our house, the daytime fast was traditionally broken with lentil soup (see page 116) and sambusak (see pages 71 and 74). Salads and main dishes followed, and my mother tried to serve everyone's favorite dishes, including fatteh (bread with yogurt and, in our case, shredded chicken and nuts). Ramadan was the only time of the year that food was served with special beverages, and this was a sign of the importance of hydration after a time of fasting. Most beverage recipes in this book are, for me, inseparable from that special Ramadan feeling. The same holds for desserts. Desserts were primarily served for Ramadan in our family, and, insofar as I know, in most Syrian homes. And coffee—there is nothing like the taste of coffee after a long day of fasting . . . Divine.

As a kid, I would spend more time in the kitchen during Ramadan than any other time of the year. I would sit in a chair, watching everything my mother did as part of her days in the kitchen. I would distract her with my made-up stories, each one more fantastical than the last, in the hope that she would let me sit there for just a little bit longer. Or, better yet, in the hope that she would let me help. She inevitably shooed me away to go do "boy stuff," but I did everything I could to postpone that moment. I'll never forget the amused smile on my mother's lips while she listened. It was the smile of Ramadan.

Qamar al-deen
— Apricot and Orange Blossom Juice with Pine Nuts

Break the sheets of apricot leather into small pieces and place them in a heat-safe bowl. Cover with the boiling water and soak for 15 minutes until soft.

In a blender, purée the softened apricots together with the soaking water and the orange blossom water. Blend until the drink has the consistency of a smoothie.

Pour into a large pitcher and refrigerate for at least 2 hours. Serve the drink with a lot of ice. Garnish with some raw pine nuts sprinkled on top.

INGREDIENTS

SERVES 4

14 oz (400 g) of apricot leather sheets
   (dried apricot paste sheets, or qamar al-deen)
3½ cups (800 ml) of boiling water
1 teaspoon of orange blossom water

TO SERVE
Ice cubes
Small handful of raw pine nuts
—
Blender

Fruit leather is available everywhere in Syria, making it no wonder that it is regularly called for in recipes. This apricot drink is an example, and one where the flavor is extra-intense and the texture is unique. You can find the thick fruit leather in well-stocked Middle Eastern shops. Qamar al-deen should not be missing from the Ramadan table.

Mbatan
— Rice Pudding with Apricot Syrup

PREPARATION

In a large saucepan, combine the rice and measured water. Cook, stirring constantly, over medium heat for 10 minutes, until the water is absorbed.

Add the milk, rose water, sugar, and cornstarch and cook the rice, stirring constantly, for another 5 minutes, until the sugar has dissolved and the pudding is thick.

Divide the pudding evenly among little bowls or glasses. Cool in the refrigerator.

While the pudding is cooling, prepare the half-quantity of Qamar al-deen, if you have not already. Omit the pine nuts from the recipe.

For the apricot syrup, mix the cornstarch with the measured water in a little cup. Heat the half-portion of qamar al-deen in a saucepan over medium heat and stir in the dissolved cornstarch. Cook, stirring constantly, until the syrup is thick and coats the spoon.

Pour a thin layer of apricot syrup over the rice pudding. Refrigerate to cool completely. Serve the mbatan cold, topped with some pistachios.

INGREDIENTS

SERVES 6

1⅔ cups (125 g) of risotto or short-grain rice (rinsed)
1⅔ cups (400 ml) of cool water
3½ cups (800 ml) of whole milk
1 teaspoon of rose water
¼ cup (50 g) of sugar
Scant ½ cup (50 g) of cornstarch
2 tablespoons of chopped pistachios

FOR THE APRICOT SYRUP
½ quantity of Qamar al-deen juice
   (pine nuts omitted, page 210)
2 teaspoons of cornstarch
2 tablespoons of cold water

This layered dessert is a guaranteed success at dinner parties. Serve it in small glasses to show off the exquisite layers. The apricot layer, made from dried apricot leather, is very sweet and shines in contrast with the rice pudding. I don't like things that are too sweet and so I don't add very much sugar to the pudding. You can always up the sweetness to your preference.

Ashta
— Syrian-Style Ricotta Cheese

PREPARATION

In a saucepan, heat 6¼ cups (1.5 liters) of the milk over medium heat, without letting it boil. Stir in the vinegar to curdle the milk. The curd will start to float in transparent, watery whey.

Using a slotted spoon, skim the curds out of the pan and place them in a bowl. Discard the whey.

In a large saucepan, combine the remaining 2 cups (500 ml) or so of milk and the cornstarch, and heat slowly, whisking constantly, until the milk starts to form a custard.

Whisk the curds into the custard and keep whisking for another 5 minutes, or until everything is mixed and takes on a texture similar to ricotta cheese.

Spoon the ashta into a heatproof, airtight, and sealable container.

Refrigerate for at least 2 hours to chill completely before using.

INGREDIENTS

MAKES ABOUT 3 CUPS (1 LB 12 OZ/800 G)

8½ cups (2 liters) of whole milk
¼ cup (60 ml) of white vinegar
½ cup (65 g) of cornstarch

Ashta is a creamy Middle Eastern fresh cheese and it is a key ingredient in many Syrian desserts. The cheese is almost always eaten in combination with atter (sugar syrup; see page 18), which is sweet enough on its own, so the ashta is not usually sweetened itself. If you're in a hurry, you can substitute ricotta for ashta. But, for a more authentic flavor, you really have to use homemade ashta. One of the simplest of Syrian desserts is a plate of ashta drizzled with atter and sprinkled with chopped pistachios.

Spiral shabiyat
— Filo Spiral with Ashta and Raspberry Filling

Your work surface should be clean and dry. Lay the first sheet of filo pastry in front of you horizontally. Brush the top with some of the melted butter and place a second sheet on top. Repeat so you have a triple layer.

Working quickly, spoon ½ cup (125 g) of the ashta in a thick layer across the top of the stacked filo, leaving a border of 2 inches (5 cm) on all sides. Sprinkle some of the chopped pistachios over the ashta and press a few of the raspberries into the filling, reserving some raspberries for the garnish.

Fold the bottom edge of the filo pastry over the filling to meet the top edge, using melted butter to seal them together. Gently press the pastry down around the filling. Fold in the side edges of the dough and then roll up the dough so that all the filling is completely encased in the filo roll, sealing it with melted butter. Repeat with the rest of the filo sheets and filling to make 8 long filo rolls.

Preheat the oven to 350°F (180°C). Grease a 9 inch (23 cm) round springform cake pan with some of the melted butter. Start forming the filo spiral by coiling one filo roll in the center of the springform pan. Be careful to not tear the dough, otherwise the filling will spill out while baking.

Add the other filo rolls to continue and complete the spiral, connecting the start of one roll to the end of the previous roll. You may need to tighten the spiral as you go to fit all the rolls in the pan.

Generously brush the top of the spiral with the rest of the melted butter and bake for 30–35 minutes in the oven, until golden brown and flaky.

SERVES 15

1 lb (450 g) package of filo pastry (defrosted if frozen)
2 sticks (225 g) of butter (melted)
3–3¾ cups (800 g–1 kg) of ashta (page 214)
   or whole-milk ricotta
¾ cup (100 g) of finely chopped pistachios,
   plus extra to garnish
2½ cups (300 g) of raspberries, plus extra to garnish
⅔ cup (150 ml) of atter syrup (page 18), or more to taste
—
Round springform cake pan

Remove from the oven and immediately drizzle half of the cool atter over the spiral, so that it is absorbed by the pastry. Set aside to cool to room temperature, and reserve the rest of the syrup for serving.

Decorate the shabiyat with extra pistachios and the reserved raspberries. Cut into slices and serve at room temperature, with extra atter on the side.

Just thinking of this dessert makes me happy. I'm reminded of large family gatherings or when we would entertain a large group of friends. We would order this dessert from the baklava shop. It was made in an enormous pan that probably measured 3 feet (1 meter) in diameter. The original is called "shabiyat," which is layers of filo dough and ashta (page 214) topped with nuts, then soaked in atter (page 18), and cut into small triangles. My version plays with the original a bit: the filling is made with raspberries and nuts and the layers are rolled up into a large spiral.

Walnut baklava

Baklava is the most famous pastry from the Arabic-speaking world and is popular worldwide, as it is in Syria, thanks to the Ottomans. In our family, we always have a box of baklava in the house, ready to bring out if someone comes over for a coffee.

In Syria, we buy baklava at a shop instead of making it at home. Cities are spilling with baklava shops that sell all sorts of pastries with just the right balance of crispiness and sweetness. I personally think that the baklava sold in Europe is too sweet; it detracts from the taste of the nuts. This is why I choose to make my own baklava.

(221)

Walnut baklava

Preheat the oven to 350°F (180°C).

In a food processor, grind half of the walnuts with the raisins, brown sugar, and cinnamon until a thick paste forms. Add the rest of the walnuts and then pulse them a few times so that they are distributed evenly but still somewhat chunky.

Cut twenty sheets of filo dough to fit the size of your cake pan. Grease the bottom and sides of the pan with some of the melted butter and line the bottom of the pan with 8 filo dough sheets, brushing each sheet with some melted butter before layering the next sheet on top. This will help them stick together, and will help them crisp up while baking.

Spoon half of the walnut filling onto this filo base. Spread the paste using the round part of the spoon, being careful to not tear the filo.

Stack 4 sheets of filo dough onto the filling, again brushing each sheet with butter before layering on the next sheet. Spoon the other half of the filling on top, and spread it evenly over the filo. Top the baklava with the remaining 8 sheets of filo dough, again brushing each sheet with butter before layering.

Brush the rest of the melted butter onto the top sheet and cut the baklava into your desired shapes (squares, rectangles, or diamonds). Bake for 20–25 minutes, until cooked, crispy, and evenly golden.

Remove from the oven and immediately pour half of the atter evenly over the pastries. Let the syrup soak in for 15 minutes, and then pour over the rest of the syrup. Sprinkle the baklava with chopped pistachios and set aside to cool completely before serving.

INGREDIENTS

MAKES 30–40

2½ cups (300 g) of walnut pieces
½ cup (75 g) of raisins
¼ cup (50 g) of brown sugar
2 teaspoons of ground cinnamon
1 lb (450 g) package of filo dough (defrosted if frozen)
11 tablespoons (150 g) of butter (melted)

TO SERVE
⅔ cup (150 ml) of atter syrup (page 18), or more to taste
¼ cup (25 g) of finely ground pistachios
—
Food processor
Rectangular cake pan (approx. 8 x 12 x 1½ inches/ 20 x 30 x 4 cm)

*Want to know how to buy good baklava? Pay attention to the baklava pan. If the baklava is sitting in a pool of sugar syrup, then it has been soaked too long in the syrup and is probably overly sweet and not very crispy.

Asafiri
— Pancakes with Ashta and Pistachio Filling

PREPARATION

First make the batter. In a large bowl, mix the sugar and yeast. Add the warm water and whisk until the sugar is completely dissolved and the yeast is activated.

Stir in the flour, baking powder, and rose water. Whisk until the batter is smooth and homogeneous. Cover and let the batter rest for 30 minutes.

Line a plate with parchment paper.

Grease a nonstick pan lightly with the oil and set over medium heat. Make small pancakes using 2 teaspoons of batter for each—the pancakes should measure 3 inches (8 cm) in diameter. Cook for 1–2 minutes without flipping, until little bubbles are visible. The bottom should be light brown. Transfer cooked pancakes to the lined plate and let them cool.

Fold a pancake in half and press on it hard enough to mark the crease. Spoon a tablespoon of ashta into the fold of the pancake, and sprinkle some pistachios onto the exposed ashta. Arrange on a serving platter and finish with a drizzle of atter.

INGREDIENTS

MAKES 60

FOR THE BATTER
3 tablespoons of sugar
1 envelope (7 g) of instant yeast
3 cups (700 ml) of warm water
3 cups (350 g) of all-purpose flour
1 teaspoon of baking powder
2 teaspoons of rose water
2 teaspoons of vegetable oil

FOR THE FILLING
2¼ cups (600 g) of ashta (page 214) or whole-milk ricotta
⅓ cup (50 g) of pistachios (coarsely chopped)
Atter syrup (page 18), for drizzling

These filled pancakes and qatayef (the fried version, see page 241) are made from the same batter recipe. And both are highlights on the Ramadan table (see page 207). Here, pancakes are made then filled with an ashta and pistachio filling.

Soos
— Sweet-and-Sour Licorice Beverage

PREPARATION

In a mixing bowl, combine the licorice, baking soda, and ¼ cup (60 ml) of water and rub with your fingers for 2 minutes to mix. Cover and set aside for 1 hour.

Stack your sheets of cheesecloth so you have a double- or triple-layer. Pour the contents of the bowl into the center. Gather the corners, twist them together, and knot to form a sort of tea bag.

Hang the cheesecloth tea bag in a pitcher with 4¼ cups (1 liter) water. Swish the tea bag around for 3 minutes in and out of the water in order to release as much flavor as possible.

Add the orange blossom water and serve the beverage cold, on ice.

INGREDIENTS

SERVES 6

1¾ oz (50 g) of licorice root
   (coarsely ground with a mortar and pestle)
½ teaspoon of baking soda
Water
½ teaspoon of orange blossom water
Ice cubes, to serve
—
Cheesecloth (two or three 6 x 8 inch/15 x 20 cm pieces)
Mortar and pestle

Soos is made from licorice root and tastes sweet and bitter at the same time. In Syria, the beverage is made and sold by someone called a sawaz. They are recognizable by their particular outfit and by the enormous pointed metal "teapot" they carry on their back. The sawaz walks through the city's souks with this teapot on their back and serves customers, as well as shop owners. Order a soos from them and they will pour it from as high as possible into a glass—a thin layer of foam is the sign of a good glass of soos.

Jallab
— Beverage with Molasses, Nuts, and Raisins

In a large pitcher, dissolve the grape molasses, date molasses, and rose water in the cold water. To serve, stir in the raisins and nuts, and pour into glasses with lots of ice cubes.

————

*In Syria and throughout the Middle East, pre-made jallab syrup (equal parts grape and date molasses) is sold in bottles.

SERVES 6

4 tablespoons of grape molasses
4 tablespoons of date molasses
4 tablespoons of rose water
4¼ cups (1 liter) of cold water

TO SERVE
½ cup (75 g) of golden raisins
About ⅔ cup (100 g) of nuts (pine nuts,
   pistachios, blanched almonds)
Ice cubes

This beverage is as old as it is loved. Refreshing and dark purple, it is especially popular at Ramadan (see page 207). The nuts might strike you as an unexpected—but decadent—touch. Did you know that the amount of nuts that your guest is served in their glass is a sign of your wealth and generosity?

Karkadi
— Sparkling Hibiscus Tea with Lemon Slices

PREPARATION

In a heat-safe pitcher, pour boiling the water over the hibiscus flowers and steep for 10–15 minutes. Strain the tea and refrigerate until cold.

Mix the hibiscus tea with the sparkling water, rose water, and lemon slices. Add honey if desired and then serve the tea with a generous amount of ice cubes. Garnish with dried rose petals, if desired.

INGREDIENTS

SERVES 6

1⅔ cups (400 ml) of boiling water
1¾ oz (50 g) of dried hibiscus flowers
2 cups (500 ml) of sparkling water
2 tablespoons of rose water
1 organic lemon (thinly sliced)
Honey (as desired)

TO SERVE
Ice cubes
Dried rose petals (optional)

This popular hibiscus flower tea is not only drunk in Syria, but throughout the Arab world—even in Egypt. Egyptians drink it during holidays; we Syrians borrowed this tradition and serve it primarily during Ramadan (see page 207). My sparkling version is served with lemon slices. Refreshingly delicious.

Aish el saraya
— Ashta and Caramel Bread "Cheesecake"

PREPARATION

Toast the slices of bread in a toaster or under the broiler. Break the toast into pieces and, working in batches, pulse them for 20 seconds in a food processor until they are fine crumbs.

In a wide pan, dissolve the sugar in the water over medium heat. Continue to cook the sugar solution for 10–15 minutes until it starts to bubble and caramelize to a golden brown.

As soon as the caramel syrup is golden brown, add the butter and stir until it is completely melted. Remove from the heat.

Stir the breadcrumbs into the caramel sauce so that all the crumbs are coated. It should look like a thick paste. Keep stirring, adding some water if needed, until all the breadcrumbs are incorporated.

Grease your springform cake pan. Turn the caramel crumbs into the bottom of the greased pan. Spread the crumbs evenly, pressing on them with the rounded side of a spoon, to form a base, ½ inch (1 cm) thick. Spoon the ashta on top of the caramel and then smooth it using the round side of a spoon.

Refrigerate the saraya for at least 3 hours.* Release the sides of the springform pan and remove. Garnish the dessert as desired with pistachios and rose jam. Drizzle liberally with atter syrup and serve the slices with extra atter on the side.

———

*You can also make this dessert ahead of time and keep it refrigerated for 2–3 days.

INGREDIENTS

SERVES 8

10 slices of white bread
¾ cup (150 g) of sugar
Generous ¾ cup (200 ml) of water
2 tablespoons (30 g) of butter, plus extra for greasing
1¼ cups (300 g) of ashta (page 214) or whole-milk ricotta

TO SERVE
2 tablespoons of pistachios (very finely chopped)
2 tablespoons of rose jam (as desired)
Atter syrup (page 18)
—
Food processor
Round springform cake pan
  (8½ inches/22 cm in diameter)

"Aish" means "bread" in Egyptian Arabic, and "saraya" means "palace." This breadcrumb dessert has a regal allure. Just like so many other Syrian desserts, it is made with ashta (page 214), atter (page 18), and nuts.

Karawiyah
— Caraway Pudding with Nuts and Grated Coconut

In a saucepan, mix the rice with the sugar, caraway, and cinnamon. Add the water and cook over medium heat for 15 minutes, stirring constantly so that the rice doesn't stick to the bottom of the pan. Turn the heat to low as soon as the rice starts to bubble. Continue cooking for another 5 minutes, stirring constantly, until the rice is completely cooked.

Cool for 30 minutes and purée the cooked rice in the food processor or blender for 1 minute. It should be smooth and creamy.

Divide the rice among 4 glasses or bowls and cool completely. Refrigerate for at least 1 hour, until firm.

Finish with a sprinkling of grated coconut and nuts.

SERVES 4

½ cup (100 g) of white rice
¼ cup (50 g) of sugar
2 tablespoons of ground caraway seeds
1 tablespoon of ground cinnamon
3½ cups (800 ml) of water

TO SERVE
Grated coconut
Pine nuts
Chopped pistachios
—
Food processor or blender

This smooth rice pudding, made with caraway seeds and served with a layer of nuts and grated coconut, is traditionally served at baby showers. Many a baby's birth has been celebrated with this dessert!

Kaak
— Cookies with a Sesame–Anise Glaze

In a large bowl, whisk together the milk, sugar, oil, and egg until smooth and homogeneous.

In another bowl, combine the flour, semolina, cornstarch, salt, vanilla bean paste, baking powder, and anise seeds. Gradually whisk the milk mixture into the dry ingredients until it is completely incorporated. The dough should be soft and sticky. Cover and set aside for 1 hour.

After the dough has rested, it should have a smooth consistency and should not feel sticky anymore.

To form the cookies, divide the dough into apricot-sized balls and roll them into little sausages about 8 inches (20 cm) long. Join the ends to form rings about 2 inches (5 cm) in diameter.

Preheat the oven to 350°F (180°C). Line a baking sheet with parchment paper.

Make the crust: Whisk the egg, milk, and vinegar together and pour it into a shallow dish. Mix the sesame and anise seeds in another dish. Dip the cookie base into the egg mixture and then into the seed mixture. Arrange the kaak, seed side up, on the prepared pan. Bake for 20–30 minutes, until golden brown.

After baking, cool the cookies for at least 30 minutes before dipping them into a cup of tea.

MAKES 12–15

FOR THE COOKIES
5 tablespoons of milk
⅓ cup (65 g) of sugar
¼ cup (60 ml) of vegetable oil
1 egg
1¼ cups (155 g) of all-purpose flour
½ cup (90 g) of semolina
Scant ½ cup (50 g) of cornstarch
½ teaspoon of salt
½ teaspoon of vanilla bean paste
½ teaspoon of baking powder
1 tablespoon of anise seeds

FOR THE CRUST
1 egg
2 tablespoons of milk
1 tablespoon of vinegar
3 tablespoons of sesame seeds
1 teaspoon of anise seeds

These cookies resemble old-fashioned Dutch cookies in more than name only. Syrians, like the Dutch, eat their kaak with coffee or tea. They are usually sold ready-made at specialty shops in Syria. My grandmother somehow discovered an amazing cookie shop that had their storefront along the highway connecting Damascus to Homs, which ran past the airport. Every time a family member flew into that airport, my grandmother would order a couple of kilograms of cookies, ready for pick-up. This treat gives me a warm, homey, winter feeling.

Forgotten date cake

PREPARATION

Preheat the oven to 350°F (180°C).

Place the dates in a small heatproof bowl and pour the boiling water over them. The dates should be completely covered. Soak for 15 minutes.

In a food processor, blend the dates and their soaking water for 30 seconds, or until the dates are finely chopped. The texture should not be completely smooth.

In a bowl, use a hand mixer to beat together the eggs, oil, milk, vanilla extract, and brown sugar for 2–3 minutes until well combined, light in color, and fluffy.

Using a rubber spatula, carefully fold the date pieces into the egg mixture. In a separate bowl, sift the flour, cinnamon, baking powder, and baking soda, whisk to mix, and then fold into the egg mixture.

Line the bottom and sides of an 8 inch (20 cm) cake pan with parchment paper. Pour the batter into the pan and bake in the middle of the oven for 30 minutes, or until a skewer inserted into the center comes out clean.

While the cake is baking, make the caramel: In a large nonstick pan, heat the sugar without stirring, over medium heat, just until it begins to melt and caramelize at the sides of the pan. Now you can carefully swirl the pan to mix. As soon as the sugar starts to become liquid and turn golden brown, add the butter. The caramel will start to bubble and spatter. Do not stand too close!

Stir the caramel with a wooden spoon until the butter is completely melted, and then, stirring constantly,

INGREDIENTS

SERVES 8

1½ cups (200 g) of soft pitted dates
1 cup (225 ml) of boiling water
2 eggs
½ cup (125 ml) of vegetable oil
3½ tablespoons of milk
1 teaspoon of vanilla extract
¼ packed cup (50 g) of brown sugar
2 cups (250 g) of all-purpose flour
1 teaspoon of ground cinnamon
1 teaspoon of baking powder
1 teaspoon of baking soda

FOR THE CARAMEL SAUCE
1 cup (200 g) of sugar
3 tablespoons (45 g) of butter
½ cup (125 ml) of heavy cream
½ teaspoon of salt
—
Food processor or blender
Hand mixer
8 inch (20 cm) round springform or square cake pan

pour in the cream. Continue cooking the caramel for 2–3 minutes until it thickens. When the caramel starts to coat the back of the spoon, add the salt. Stir to mix, remove from the heat, and let the caramel cool.

Take the cake out of the oven and cool for at least 30 minutes before taking it out of the cake pan.

Place the cooled cake on a cake stand and drizzle with the caramel sauce.

This recipe is my mother's invention and is truly a fusion dish, thanks to the dates that are ubiquitous in Saudi cuisine. When I asked my mother for the recipe, she didn't even remember having created this cake. She was convinced that it was one of her friends' recipes! It was only after a friend found a recipe from decades ago, written in my mother's handwriting, that she believed that this recipe was hers. Perfect for coffee or dessert.

Qatayef
— Mini-Pancakes with Ashta and Walnut Filling

First make the batter. In a large bowl, mix the sugar and yeast. Add the warm water and whisk until the sugar is fully dissolved and the yeast is activated. Stir in the flour, baking powder, and rose water. Whisk until the batter is smooth and homogeneous. Cover and let the batter rest for 30 minutes.

Line a plate with paper towels.

Grease a nonstick frying pan lightly with oil and set it over medium heat. Make small pancakes using 2 tablespoons of batter for each—they should measure 4 inches (10 cm) in diameter. Cook for 1–2 minutes without flipping and until little bubbles are visible. The bottom should be light brown. Transfer the cooked pancakes to the lined plate.

To fill the qatayef, place a tablespoon of the ashta in the middle of each pancake. At this point, if you like, press some chopped walnuts into the ashta. Fold the pancakes over and press the edges together firmly to seal them.

Add enough oil to the frying pan to cover the bottom to a depth of ½ an inch (1 cm). Heat the oil until hot but not smoking (test-fry one qatayef—the oil should immediately start to bubble around the qatayef). Fry the qatayef in batches, for 20–30 seconds on each side, until crispy, topping up the oil as needed. The bottom of the qatayef should be completely under the oil at all times.

Transfer the qatayef to a plate lined with paper towels to drain. Arrange in a serving dish, drizzle with atter, and garnish with pistachios.

INGREDIENTS

MAKES 30

FOR THE BATTER
3 tablespoons of sugar
1 envelope (7 g) of instant yeast
3 cups (700 ml) of warm water
3 cups (350 g) of all-purpose flour
1 teaspoon of baking powder
2 teaspoons of rose water
Vegetable oil, for greasing and frying

FOR THE FILLING
1½ cups (400 g) of ashta (page 214) or whole-milk ricotta
Generous ¾ cup (100 g) of chopped walnuts (optional)

TO SERVE
Atter syrup (page 18)
3 tablespoons of pistachios (coarsely chopped)

This visually-pleasing dessert is very similar to asafiri (page 225), only the filled pancakes are formed into half-moons and fried. Ashta (page 214) is a Syrian fresh cheese and is like a mixture of ricotta and cottage cheese. Ricotta is an excellent substitute.

Index

—

A

Apricot and Orange Blossom Juice with
    Pine Nuts   (210)
Apricot Syrup, Rice Pudding with   (213)
Ashta and Caramel Bread "Cheesecake"   (233)
Aunt Jinan's Bulgur Salad   (119)

B

Baked Eggplant and Ground Beef in Tomato
    Sauce   (146)
beef
    Beef Sausage with Garlic and Pistachios   (079)
    Beef shawarma   (093)
    Beef Stew with Green Peas   (145)
    Eggplant and Beef Pilaf   (151)
    Eggs with Beef and Zucchini   (052)
    Mini-Flatbreads with Ground Beef   (075)
    Roasted Eggplant Dip with Tomato–Meat Sauce   (051)
    Stew of Spinach and Ground Beef   (142)
beets
    Beet and Tahini Dip   (067)
    Mom's Famous Beet Salad   (127)
Beverage with Molasses, Nuts, and Raisins   (229)
breads
    Ashta and Caramel Bread "Cheesecake"   (233)
    Famous Toasted Bread Salad   (112)
    Flatbread with Shredded Chicken, Onions,
        and Sumac   (202)
    Flatbread with Spicy Tomato Sauce   (038)
    Mini-Flatbreads with Ground Beef   (075)
    Za'atar Flatbread   (030)
Bulgur and Meat Croquettes   (156)
Bulgur Salad, Aunt Jinan's   (119)

C

cakes
    Ashta and Caramel Bread "Cheesecake"   (233)
    Forgotten Date Cake   (238)
Caraway Pudding with Nuts and Grated Coconut   (234)
cheese
    Filo Rolls with Cheese Filling   (071)
    Syrian-Style Ricotta Cheese   (214)
    Toasted Sandwiches with Spicy Meat and Cheese   (103)
chicken
    Chicken Kofta Kebabs   (191)
    Chicken Shish Kebabs   (194)
    "Dirty" Bulgur with Roast Chicken   (197)
    Flatbread with Shredded Chicken, Onions,
        and Sumac   (202)
chickpeas
    Chickpeas in Yogurt–Tahini Sauce   (026)

"Dirty" Bulgur with Roast Chicken   (197)
    Falafel   (092)
    Hummus with Olive Oil   (061)
    Hummus with Tahini   (060)
Chili Sauce, Hot Green   (020)
Cookies with a Sesame–Anise Glaze   (237)
Cucumber, Yogurt with Garlic and   (080)

D

dips
    Beet and Tahini Dip   (067)
    Eggplant and Red Pepper Dip   (055)
    Roasted Eggplant, Yogurt, and
        Tahini Dip   (048)
    Spicy Red Pepper–Walnut Dip   (083)
"Dirty" Bulgur with Roast Chicken   (197)
drinks
    Apricot and Orange Blossom Juice with
        Pine Nuts   (210)
    Beverage with Molasses, Nuts,
        and Raisins   (229)
    Sparkling Hibiscus Tea with Lemon Slices   (230)
    Sweet-and-Sour Licorice Beverage   (226)

E

eggplants
    Baked Eggplants and Ground Beef in
        Tomato Sauce   (146)
    Eggplant and Beef Pilaf   (151)
    Eggplant Jam   (034)
    Eggplant and Red Pepper Dip   (055)
    Grilled Eggplants with Yogurt Sauce   (123)
    Roasted Eggplant Dip with
        Tomato–Meat Sauce   (051)
    Roasted Eggplant, Yogurt, and
        Tahini Dip   (048)
    Sour Eggplant   (088)
eggs
    Egg Pancakes with Parsley   (037)
    Eggs in Tomato Sauce with Chilies   (029)
    Eggs with Beef and Zucchini   (052)

F

Falafel   (092)
Famous Toasted Bread Salad   (112)
Fava Beans in Olive Oil   (033)
Filo Pastries with Meat and Rice Filling   (170)
Filo Rolls with Cheese Filling   (071)
Filo Rolls with Meat Filling   (074)
Filo Spiral with Ashta and
    Raspberry Filling   (217)

fish
  Fish in Spicy Nut Sauce   (201)
  Fish with Sumac–Tahini Sauce   (182)
  Spiced Fish Pilaf with Caramelized Onions   (188)
flatbreads   *see* breads
Forgotten Date Cake   (238)
Fresh Fava Beans with Cilantro and Garlic   (064)

G

Green Beans in Tomato and Olive Oil Sauce   (115)
Grilled Eggplants with Yogurt Sauce   (123)
Ground Beef in Tomato Sauce, Baked
    Eggplant and   (146)
Ground Beef, Stew of Spinach and   (142)

H

Hot Green Chili Sauce   (020)
Hummus with Olive Oil   (061)
Hummus with Tahini   (060)

J

juices   *see* drinks

K

Kibbeh in Mint–Yogurt Sauce   (160)
Kibbeh in Sour Tomato–Pomegranate
    Sauce   (159)
Kibbeh Tart   (163)

L

Labneh Balls   (042)
lamb
  Lamb Kebabs with Cherries   (173)
  Lamb Koftas in Tahini Sauce   (152)
  Lamb and Vegetable Kebabs with
    Khebzeh Hamra   (174)
  Tomato Soup with Barley and Lamb Shanks   (169)
lentils
  Lentil and Pasta Stew with Tamarind
    and Pomegranate   (124)
  Lentil Pilaf with Caramelized Onions   (128)
  Traditional Red Lentil Soup   (116)

M

Meat Croquettes, Bulgur and   (156)
Mini-Flatbreads with Ground Beef   (075)
Mini-Pancakes with Ashta and Walnut Filling   (241)
Mint–Yogurt Sauce, Kibbeh in   (160)
Mom's Famous Beet Salad   (127)

O

Olive Oil, Lemon, Garlic Sauce   (020)
Orange Blossom, Apricot Juice with
    Pine Nuts and   (210)

P

Pan-Fried Zucchini with Garlic and Mint   (104)
pancakes
  Egg Pancakes with Parsley   (037)
  Mini-Pancakes with Ashta and Walnut Filling   (241)
  Pancakes with Ashta and Pistachio Filling   (225)
pastry
  Filo Pastries with Meat and Rice Filling   (170)
  Filo Rolls with Cheese Filling   (071)
  Filo Rolls with Meat Filling   (074)
  Filo Spiral with Ashta and Raspberry Filling   (217)
  Walnut Baklava   (222)
peas
  Beef Stew with Green Peas   (145)
  "Dirty" Bulgur with Roast Chicken   (197)
  Filo Pastries with Meat and Rice Filling   (170)
pesto
  Parlsey–Cilantro Pesto   (021)
  Tahini–Mint Pesto   (021)
phyllo   *see* filo
pies and tarts
  Kibbeh Tart   (163)
  Spinach Pies   (068)
Pilaf with Caramelized Onions, Spicy Fish   (188)
Pudding with Nuts and Grated Coconut, Caraway   (234)

R

red peppers
  Eggplant and Red Pepper Dip   (055)
  Spicy Red Pepper–Walnut Dip   (083)
  stuffed red pepper pickles   (120)
Rice Pudding with Apricot Syrup   (213)
Roasted Eggplant, Yogurt, and Tahini Dip   (048)

S

salads
  Aunt Jinan's Bulgur Salad   (119)
  Famous Toasted Bread Salad   (112)
  Mom's Famous Beet Salad   (127)
  Simple Onion and Parsley Salad   (135)
  Watermelon, Halloumi, and Mint Salad   (198)
sauces
  Fish with Sumac–Tahini Sauce   (182)
  Flatbread with Spicy Tomato Sauce   (038)
  Grilled Eggplants with Yogurt Sauce   (123)
  Hot Green Chili Sauce   (020)
  Kibbeh in Mint–Yogurt Sauce   (160)
  Lamb Koftas in Tahini Sauce   (152)
  Olive Oil, Lemon, Garlic Sauce   (020)
  Stuffed Parsnips in Tomato Sauce   (166)
  Tahini Sauce   (021)
Shrimp with Garlic, Cilantro, and
    Cayenne Pepper   (181)
soups and stews
  Beef Stew with Green Peas   (145)

Lentil and Pasta Stew with Tamarind
and Pomegranate   (124)
Stew of Spinach and Ground Beef   (142)
Tomato Soup with Barley and Lamb Shanks   (169)
Traditional Red Lentil Soup   (116)
Sour Eggplant   (088)
Sparkling Hibiscus Tea with Lemon Slices   (230)
Spiced Fish Pilaf with Caramelized Onions   (188)
Spicy Pickles   (120)
pickled cucumbers   (120)
pickled stuffed red peppers   (120)
pickled turnips   (120)
Spicy Potatoes with Garlic and Cilantro   (056)
Spicy Red Pepper–Walnut Dip   (083)
Spicy Roasted Cauliflower   (098)
Spinach Pies   (068)
Stew of Spinach and Ground Beef   (142)
Stuffed Parsnips in Tomato Sauce   (166)
sumac
Famous Toasted Bread Salad   (112)
Flatbread with Shredded Chicken, Onions,
and Sumac   (202)
Fish with Sumac–Tahini Sauce   (182)
Simple Onion and Parsley Salad   (135)
Spinach Pies   (068)
Traditional Red Lentil Soup   (116)
Sweet-and-Sour Licorice Beverage   (226)
Swiss Chard Rolls with Rice Filling   (134)
Syrian-Style Ricotta Cheese   (214)

T
tahini
Beet and Tahini Dip   (067)
Chickpeas in Yogurt–Tahini Sauce   (026)
Fish with Sumac–Tahini Sauce   (182)
Grilled Eggplants with Yogurt Sauce   (123)
Hummus with Tahini   (060)
Lamb Koftas in Tahini Sauce   (152)
Roasted Eggplant, Yogurt, and Tahini
Dip   (048)
Tahini–Mint Pesto   (021)
Tahini Sauce   (021)
tarts   see pies and tarts
teas   see drinks
Toasted Sandwiches with Spicy Meat and Cheese   (103)
tomatoes
Baked Eggplants and Ground Beef in
Tomato Sauce   (146)
Eggs in Tomato Sauce with Chilies   (029)
Flatbread with Spicy Tomato Sauce   (038)
Green Beans in Tomato and Olive Oil
Sauce   (115)
Kibbeh in Sour Tomato–Pomegranate
Sauce   (159)
Roasted Eggplant Dip with Tomato–Meat Sauce   (051)

Stuffed Parsnips in Tomato Sauce   (166)
Tomato Soup with Barley and Lamb Shanks   (169)
Traditional Red Lentil Soup   (116)

W
walnuts
Mini-Pancakes with Ashta and Walnut Filling   (241)
Spicy Red Pepper–Walnut Dip   (083)
Walnut Baklava   (222)
Watermelon, Halloumi, and Mint Salad   (198)

Y
Yogurt Cheese   (041)
Yogurt Sauce, Grilled Eggplant with   (123)
Yogurt with Cucumber and Garlic   (080)

Z
Za'atar Flatbread   (030)
zucchini
Eggs with Beef and Zucchini   (052)
Pan-Fried Zucchini with Garlic and Mint   (104)

Acknowledgments

—

My extraordinary mother. You have inspired so incredibly many people around you. Thank you for your patience during our endless Skype and phone conversations, each of us sitting in our respective kitchens.

Basma, my sister, my best friend. You have been an inspiration and positive force in my life since we were kids. Thank you for listening, thinking along, and challenging me. Thanks to you, I have been able to be the best version of myself. Thanks also to your sweet and beautiful family.

Dad, you're no longer here physically, but your goodness and love will be forever in my mind and heart. I love you.

Haya, my little sister in action. You were able to think outside the box so that this book could become all that it is. Thank you.

Jacob. Thank you for your amazing support and patience during this project and for all the other weird plans I came up with every day. Thank you for being my advisor, a shoulder to lean on, the recipe guinea pig, and my friend. A huge thank you to the Roex family for all your support.

Hadi, the brother that I never had. You are a wonderful head chef, you have a special irreverence for all the norms and rules, and you create beautiful, delicious culinary creations. Thank you for your help; there is no part of this book that doesn't bear your influence.

To all my friends throughout the world: from Italy to Germany, from Syria to Lebanon and Saudi Arabia, from North America to Russia. You know who you are. You are way too many to name. Thank you.

To the "Ghawali" family, my dear family members with whom I kept contact via WhatsApp. To my aunt in Germany, whose traditional Syrian tablecloths I ordered to use for the photo shoots. And to my aunt in Syria, who shipped me her collection of authentic cookware, serving dishes, and utensils. All these recipes and stories in this book are inspired by you as well.

Rania, thank you for letting me use the beautiful photographs of your beloved city Damascus. They enrich this book and give it life. Thanks to you, we see that current-day Syria is not a country only associated with war, violence, and destruction.

To the "A team," Maaike, Ajda, Suzanne, and Jeroen. Thank you for all your hard work. You are wonderful; the best team I could wish for. I will miss working with all of you.

Thank you, Miriam, Sofie, and the whole team at publisher Nijgh Cuisine, and my English-language publishers Murdoch Books and Interlink Publishing. You believed in my idea. We made it!

First published in 2021 by

INTERLINK BOOKS
An imprint of Interlink Publishing Group, Inc.
46 Crosby Street
Northampton, Massachusetts 01060
www.interlinkbooks.com

For our complete catalog visit out website at
www.interlinkbooks.com or e-mail:
sales@interlinkbooks.com

Recipes: Anas Atassi and Ajda Mehmet

Text: Anas Atassi and Suzanne Stougie

Food photography: Jeroen van der Spek

Location photography in Syria: Rania Kataf,
  with the exception of the family photographs
  from the private collection of Anas Atassi.

**Creative direction, photography,
  and styling:** Maaike Koorman

Food styling: Ajda Mehmet

Cover design: Annelies Dollekamp

Graphic design: Janine Kopatz

Executive designer: Annelies Dollekamp

Editors: Yulia Knol and Marte Steendam

With thanks to, Nathalie Hildesheim of Piece of Clay,
  for making beautiful ceramics; Zenza, for the use of
  glassware and the round tile table, zenzahome.com;
  Van Dijk and Ko for their collaboration,
  vandijkenko.nl; and Restaurant As for their
  hospitality.

Publisher: Corinne Roberts
American edition publisher: Michel Moushabeck
Translator: Margie Franzen
English-language editor: Elena Gomez
American edition editor: Leyla Moushabeck
English-language designer: Susanne Geppert

Text © Anas Atassi, 2019

Library of Congress Cataloging-in-Publication
Data available

ISBN 978-1-62371-897-8

Printed in China by C & C Offset Printing Co., Ltd.